Aaron Shearer

CLASSIC GUITAR TECHNIQUE

THIRD EDITION · By Aaron Shearer and Thomas Kikta

Volume 1

Alfred Publishing Co., Inc.
16320 Roscoe Blvd., Suite 100
P.O. Box 10003
Van Nuys, CA 91410-0003
alfred.com

D1212426

ISBN-10: 0-7390-5710-3 (Book & CD)
ISBN-13: 978-0-7390-5710-0 (Book & CD)

Contents

Preface

The decision to update this book, which was first published almost 50 years ago, came slowly because of its persistent popularity among beginning and intermediate students. Recognition of this more-or-less consistent popularity prompts the question of why this update is necessary. The explanation rests on my sense of responsibility to provide teachers and students with accurate information about learning to play the classic guitar, which is the reason the book has remained quite popular among teachers and students. This situation speaks mostly to the fact that many teachers have learned how to use the good information contained in the book while personally providing essential information missing in the text.

Given the environment in which the book was born, the need for updating should not come as much of a surprise. It was written by a primarily self-taught guitarist and teacher whose information was almost entirely the result of much sincere personal experimentation guided by reason and intuition. The method books available at that time, and the results of teaching I found in well-known studios in Washington D.C., Baltimore, Philadelphia, New York, and other cities, did not provide the example for the kind of instruction book I had in mind. Nor did my modest efforts towards improvement receive much encouragement from the prominent guitarists of that time. For example, Andres Segovia, after reading my manuscript, had this to say about my efforts: "Mr. Shearer, what I have to tell you, pains me much. What you have written is worthless." Of course, I was crushed! But as my visit ended and I walked down the stairway from his apartment, I pulled my wits together enough to think, why should he know? He's a great performer, not an experienced teacher; understanding this distinction has served me well over the years. Exceptional performers are not necessarily good teachers.

To report a more cheerful ending to this episode of getting the book published, I soon contacted a long-time acquaintance, Mr. Vladimir Bobri, president of the New York Guitar Society. Through his kind efforts, G. Ricordi & Co. Music Publishers agreed to accept the manuscript for publication, and within a few years, this book and its supplements became the most widely used guitar method throughout the United States and, perhaps, the world. Its success led directly to an invitation from the Peabody Conservatory in Baltimore to initiate a guitar program. My growth as an analyst of performance problems sharpened as a result of being challenged by numerous talented young students as well as from dealing with a serious attack of what I now refer to as "Repetitive Strain Injury." I became aware that, along with its many very useful instructions, *Classic Guitar Technique,* Vol. 1, contained some erroneous technical information.

Naturally, the thought of updating it crossed my mind often; however, in order to get a book published, it's customary for the writer to sign away rights of ownership to the publisher, and the publisher could not be expected to grant permission to update a book that already sells well. That, however, is exactly what the new owner has done, with the understanding that the updating will not change the appealing character of the original book, but rather the correction will make the text far more valuable to both teacher and student as a study guide.

Advancing years have made it essential to turn the job of updating over to my former student and excellent guitarist-teacher (and gifted sound engineer) Professor Thomas Kikta, who has been head of the Classic Guitar Department at Duquesne University in Pittsburgh, Pennsylvania, for more than 20 years. In addition to updating the text, Professor Kikta has added an invaluable CD for experiencing the musical selections in *Classic Guitar Technique,* Vol. 1.

Aaron Shearer

Working with a Qualified Teacher

A qualified teacher is of paramount importance when beginning to learn the guitar or wanting to advance one's abilities on the instrument. With that being said, how does one evaluate a teacher as being "qualified"? One of the first criteria to which most students gravitate is how well the teacher plays. But just because a teacher plays well does not mean he or she has the foundation to effectively teach. Many fine players have devoted their thinking to playing and not necessarily to the analytical skills required to break a subject down into small, easily understood steps as required for teaching.

In no way, shape, or form should you try to proceed without a teacher. Though the information found in this book is of extreme importance, only a qualified teacher can give you the guidance, feedback, and support to efficiently proceed with your studies.

Here are some points that you, the student, should consider when trying to determine if a teacher is qualified:

1. A qualified teacher will have a balanced curriculum that includes such subjects as seating position, guitar technique for both hands, music theory, reading, and practice techniques, as well as repertoire, phrasing, and performance. If the teacher focuses only on repertoire and phrasing and tends to sidestep issues of technique and how to use your hands, then you are not getting a balanced experience.

2. A teacher who tends to throw contrasting information at you and tells you to decide what is best is doing you a disservice, since you do not yet have the necessary foundation to make such decisions.

3. A qualified teacher will give you reasons as to why you are moving a certain way or doing what you do. Teaching by rote and saying "that's how I do it" is not good enough.

4. If a teacher does not teach by the principles in this book, then find a teacher who does. The basic principles outlined in this book are foundational and proven with time. A deviation from them is counter-productive.

5. A qualified teacher will emphasis performance as the primary goal of guitar study. The act of sharing one's music with others is the reason we play. Many students become discouraged when they are only able to play securely when they are alone. Constantly reinforcing positive habits for performing with security and confidence is essential to your progress.

Realize that an incompetent teacher is going to waste your time. If you have not made reasonable progress despite your best efforts, then perhaps it is time to find a new teacher.

About the Guitar

The Types of Guitar

At the present time, there are two widely used, though distinctly different, fretted instruments with the name "guitar." In view of this often perplexing situation, this article describing the guitar types has been included. Three points of interest are of special significance:

1. The existence of two types of guitar is confusing to an individual who has heard a guitar and decided to study the instrument. Authentic and unbiased information regarding the different types of guitars and their potential uses is frequently unavailable. The interested person, therefore, has no clear idea what type of instrument to obtain or what kind of instruction to seek.

2. It is the author's firm belief that a student of the classic guitar will benefit considerably from acquiring knowledge of the qualifications and limitations of both types, and the serious student should be able to discuss the primary differences intelligently. Occasionally, an avid enthusiast of the classic guitar asserts or implies that the plectrum guitar lacks merit as an instrument and cannot accurately be called a "guitar." Such an unrealistic attitude naturally tends to do harm by causing resentment. It must be recognized and accepted that the plectrum type is known to millions of people in both Europe and America as a "guitar." It is true that the plectrum instrument is vastly different from the classic guitar in construction, use, and performance method. There can be no question that neither guitar is superior as a solo instrument for the performance of fine, highly expressive music. One type cannot replace the other; they are simply different instruments serving different purposes. Though most of the techniques used on the classic guitar are applicable on the plectrum or steel string guitar, an excellent performer on one type could not play the other well without years of serious study. The merit of the music produced upon either type is entirely a matter of personal opinion and must be left to the unpredictable human element of individual taste.

3. The average listener, impressed with the unusual fullness and beauty emanating from the classic guitar, is often interested in learning how its characteristics differ from those of the plectrum type, and the following is a concise and accurate discussion of the subject.

The Classic Guitar

The first type of guitar to appear on the musical scene was the *classic guitar*, also known as the *Spanish guitar*, *concert guitar*, or *fingerstyle guitar*. This instrument, and the technique of playing it, are described in detail later. The classic guitar is generally used to play solo recitals and concerts with orchestral accompaniment.

The name "classical" guitar has misled many initially interested individuals into believing the instrument is only suitable for classical music; certainly, this is an incorrect impression. The description "classic" more properly derives from the instrument's enduring interest and value, from being in the first rank of instruments, rather than from any rigid association with a particular type of music. The guitar can not be confined to a single type of music any more than the piano; both are harmonic instruments, their greatness unquestionably culminating in the performance of classical music. Because of their excellence in playing fine music, it is only reasonable to assume that both the classic guitar and the piano are adaptable to less complicated forms.

The association of the classic guitar with Spain is justified because of its centuries of popularity there. To refer to the instrument as a "Spanish guitar," however, would erroneously limit its interest and acceptance as a major musical instrument. At no time during its long history, which dates back to the 11th century, has the development and use of the guitar been strictly confined to one country. Recent studies reveal conclusive evidence that the guitar was not invented by Spaniards, but was developed from the ancient Greek *kithara* by Provencals circa 1000 A.D., and had only four strings. The old six-string *vihuela*, so widely used in Spain for centuries before the advent of the modern guitar, is now recognized as a development of the Provencal instrument. (The European lute is sometimes mentioned in connection with the origin of the guitar. While both are plucked instruments, they are not related in basic construction or by name.) Whether or not the modern guitar is a development of the vihuela in Spain is not known, but it is recorded that the instrument was being used and developed in other European countries at the same time it was gaining prominence. In approximately 1788, a German craftsman named Jacob Otto added a sixth string to the then-popular five-string guitar. It should be noted that some of the finest guitars ever produced have come from Germany, and excellent instruments have been constructed in Spain and other countries as well. Many ordinary features of the modern classic guitar, such as the loop bridge, width of fingerboard, and customary inner construction, were established in Spain about 150 years ago; but for the same reason the violin is not called the "Italian violin" simply because its general characteristics were established by Italian craftsmen, the guitar should be recognized as an international instrument that is at home in the many lands and cultures of the world.

Prior to 1946, the classic guitar was strung with three plain strings made of gut and three strings made of spun silk wound with fine wire. Strings made since then are immeasurably superior and produced using a synthetic material (usually nylon) instead of gut and silk. Synthetic strings rarely break, and they remain in tune over a long period of time once thoroughly stretched. The construction of the classic guitar has also been considerably improved over the past hundred years. Despite its advancements, however, the classic guitar remains a delicate instrument, unsuitable for playing "rhythm" in the modern rock band where great volume is required. It is a highly expressive instrument, at its best where sustained harmonies, richness, and variety of tone are most sought. It is an excellent solo and accompaniment instrument, whether played in a concert hall for a large audience or in the intimacy of one's own study room for the sole benefit and enjoyment of the performer.

Fig. 1: The Classic Guitar

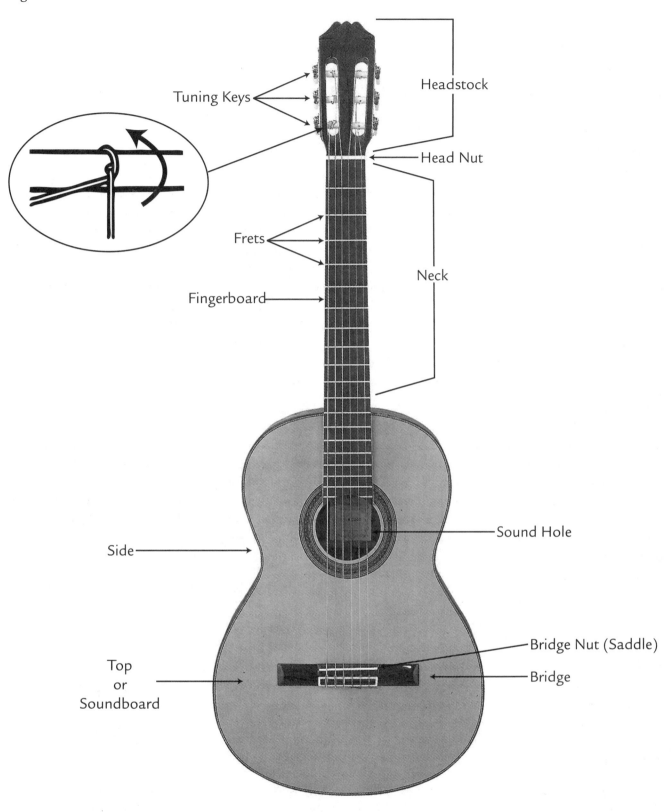

Tuning Keys

Headstock

Head Nut

Frets

Neck

Fingerboard

Sound Hole

Side

Bridge Nut (Saddle)

Top
or
Soundboard

Bridge

Below are the two customary methods of securing a string to the bridge.
Important: The turn of the string completing the knot must be behind
the back edge of the bridge. The author prefers method No. 1 for all six strings.

No. 1   No. 2

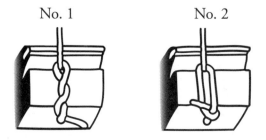

The Plectrum Guitar

The second type of guitar does not have an established descriptive name to distinguish it from the classic guitar. It is sometimes called the *plectrum guitar, pickstyle guitar, steel string guitar, American jazz guitar, folk guitar, rock guitar,* or *rhythm guitar* (though it is not necessarily restricted to playing "rhythm" or strumming). It is most incorrectly referred to as the "Spanish guitar," since the classic guitar is the type most widely used in Spain.

The plectrum guitar is specially constructed to withstand the tremendous tension of its six steel strings, which are tuned the same as those of the classic guitar. Ordinarily, the first two strings are plain steel, and the remaining four are steel wound with an alloy wire. An oval or triangular shaped *plectrum* (pick) of tortoise shell or similar material, held between the thumb and index finger of the right hand, is used to sound the strings. Employment of this single device in playing the plectrum guitar sets serious limitations upon the instrument. For example, most well-arranged music, either accompaniment or solo, requires notes to be sounded simultaneously upon widely separated strings; use of the plectrum renders this difficult. Melody with supporting harmony that lends fullness and color to a composition can only be produced with strums that include the melody note in a quick arpeggiation. This type of guitar, therefore, is usually used with one or more additional instruments when playing an accompaniment or solo. It can be played with the fingers just like the classic guitar, and is then referred to as a *fingerstyle guitar.*

The plectrum guitar is excellent as a *rhythm* instrument, working, as is customary, with bass and drums to set the beat of the modern studio or rock band. (In this type of accompaniment, the correct resolution of chord tones is relatively unimportant.) It produces a brilliant, rather metallic tone, which, in addition to being suitable for rhythm section work, is also used by Western and bluegrass singers in playing simple accompaniments. When amplified electronically (then called an *electric guitar*), it is most effective as a *melody* instrument, usually playing a single note at a time, but also acting as the rhythm instrument. The electric type of plectrum guitar is widely used as a medium for playing various types of modern jazz, popular music, rock, and Western-style music.

Note that the information provided here is not meant as an exhaustive appraisal of the guitar played with a plectrum. The intent, rather, is to furnish the reader with concise, authentic information regarding the characteristics and customary uses of the instrument.

Flamenco

Only the classic type guitar is used in the performance of flamenco music. The true "flamenco guitar," however, differs slightly from the classic guitar in its inner construction, and it is usually built of lighter wood. It was originally used and developed in Spain, primarily as an accompaniment for singing or dancing. Now, performance of flamenco music with solo guitar has developed into what may be considered a fine art.

Most authorities agree that the best approach to flamenco technique is through careful study of basic classic guitar technique. Because of the unusual and striking effects required to perform true flamenco music, the playing technique is necessarily somewhat different; however, the **basic** technique of playing the classic guitar, correctly applied, remains the same whether the instrument is used for classical, popular, or flamenco music.

Choosing a Guitar Type

Interested individuals often ask which type of guitar is more difficult to play. The author, having studied both types, finds it impossible to say which is positively more difficult. Each presents its individual problems, especially as the student reaches more advanced stages of playing. The difficulty involved in playing either type of guitar depends entirely upon the extent of the student's aspirations. It is comparatively easy to play simple chords or melodies upon either type, but several years of serious study are required to become an accomplished guitarist in either case.

It should be noted that, whether playing the classic guitar or performing fingerstyle on a steel string or electric guitar, the right hand technique is primarily identical. The benefits acquired in learning the classic guitar will create a strong foundation for approaching complex repertoire performed on a steel string instrument.

For beginning students, the classic guitar is unquestionably more rewarding and, in fact, easier to play. As noted in this book, surprisingly melodic and full-sounding little solos may be played after only a few hours of good study. The reason for this is that the classic guitar, played with the thumb and fingers of the right hand, permits the execution of widely spaced harmonies of two or more simultaneous notes. It is easier to play simply because the strings are softer and more flexible than steel strings, resulting in less irritation to the left fingertips.

The question of which instrument is more difficult to play is relatively unimportant. The first consideration for the student is which type of guitar will bring the most personal satisfaction and more fully satisfy the individual's taste.

The Playing Condition of a Guitar

The playing condition of the guitar a student intends to use is an important factor to consider. If the instrument has a warped neck or has not been properly adjusted, it will be difficult to play, if not entirely unplayable. The few minutes required for determining the playing condition of a guitar may save the student many hours of unrewarding study and considerable expense.

Before the playing condition of any guitar can be accurately tested, the instrument must first be tuned to conventional pitch. (See page 12 for tuning information.)

To test a guitar for a warped or bent neck, depress the 1st string (E) at the 1st and 15th frets simultaneously. With the string held firmly in this manner, it should appear *almost to touch* each intervening fret. The same procedure must be followed with the 6th string (E). If either string does not practically touch each intervening fret, the neck is warped. Replacing the fingerboard and/or resetting the neck may be necessary before the guitar can be considered for use.

Next in consideration is the *action* of the guitar, which, from the standpoint of playability, is of utmost importance. If the strings are high over the fingerboard, the performer will experience difficulty in pressing them firmly against the frets; the instrument is then referred to as having a "high" or "hard" action. If the strings are low over the fingerboard, they more easily produce harsh, unpleasant buzzing sounds when played; this is referred to as a "low" or "soft" action. A guitar suffering an extreme of either condition is difficult, if not impossible, to play; the action is said to be "out of adjustment." The most desirable adjustment is one in which the action is neither too high nor too low; in other words, the strings will not be too hard to press firmly against the frets, but will produce a clear tone with maximum volume. Excellent materials and craftsmanship have no bearing upon whether or not a guitar is "well adjusted." Many new guitars, even some expensive instruments, are not in good playing condition because they have not been properly adjusted; however, any guitar that has been constructed with reasonable care and does not have a warped neck can usually be adjusted quite simply by raising or lowering its bridge nut and/or head nut.

The most accurate method of determining whether or not the action is in reasonably good adjustment is to measure the distance of the strings above the frets:

1. The first step in measuring the action is to determine if the **bridge nut** is set at the correct height.
    a. With the 1st string **held firmly** against the **1st fret**, the distance between the string and the **top of the 12th fret** should be approximately 3/32 (.094) inch, no less. (See the paragraph at the top of the following page.)
    b. Measuring in the same manner as above, the 6th string should be approximately 1/8 (.125) inch, no less.
    c. The 2nd, 3rd, 4th, and 5th strings must be on a *level plane* between the 1st and 6th. (The heavy strings should have the higher action because of their wide vibrations.)
2. The final step in measuring the action is to determine if the **head nut** is set at the correct height. A standard leaf or gap gauge inserted between the strings and fret provides an excellent measuring device.
    a. With strings in an *open* position, the distance between the first two strings (E and B) and the top of the 1st fret should be 1/40 (.025) inch.
    b. The four remaining strings (3rd, 4th, 5th, and 6th) should be 1/32 (.03) inch above the 1st fret.

If action adjustment is required, it is recommended that the guitar be taken to a qualified stringed instrument repairman for correction.

The foregoing specifications produce a medium-low action suitable for the average student. As the student's playing ability and knowledge of the guitar develop, a slightly higher action may be desired, such as 1/8 inch instead of 3/32 inch under item l(a), and 5/32 inch instead of 1/8 inch under item l(b). (It may be observed that, in certain comparatively rare instances, an even lower action than that specified under item 1 is used; this is not recommended for students of the classic guitar.) Fine points of action adjustment are decided in accordance with the performer's individual requirements and in conformation with the characteristics of a particular instrument.

Care of the Guitar

Concerning general care of the guitar, students often inquire how to minimize the chances of the instrument cracking, the finish becoming marred or checked, and the neck warping. First, it must be emphasized that reputable manufacturers only guarantee their guitars against faulty materials and workmanship and not against improper care or the unpredictable nature of wood itself. Obviously, this places considerable responsibility upon the owner to treat a good guitar as the rather delicate and sensitive instrument it is.

The following are some of the most important points in the proper care of the guitar:

1. Never subject a guitar to sudden extreme changes in temperature or humidity, or to direct sunshine.

2. If the guitar must be kept in a steam-heated room, keep a container of water on the radiator and a humidifier in the guitar case.

3. Never tune the guitar to a higher pitch than standard A-440 (see p. 12). If the six strings are tuned even slightly high, a dangerous amount of unnecessary strain is exerted upon the whole instrument, including the neck and bridge.

4. Alcohol, acids from food, and even perspiration can mar the finish. Keep the finish clean, and frequently apply a good polish sold by any recognized guitar manufacturer.

The possibility that the guitar may crack will be considerably lessened by following the advice offered in items 1 and 2 above. The reader must remember, however, that all wooden instruments—violins, woodwinds, and pianos, as well as guitars—sometimes crack regardless of quality or care given. Generally, the appearance of a crack in a guitar constitutes no grave damage if given proper and immediate attention. The instrument should simply be taken to a qualified guitar or violin repairman to be fixed before the crack widens or lengthens. Rarely, if ever, does a repaired crack detract in the least from the tone, response, playability, or (to any serious degree) appearance of the instrument.

Tuning the Guitar

Obtaining the assistance of a qualified teacher or musician (not necessarily a guitarist) when attempting to tune the guitar is strongly recommended for the beginning student with no prior musical training.

Much practice is required to tune the guitar quickly and accurately. The ear must be trained to hear the slightest difference in pitch; this can be accomplished only through patiently learning to focus concentration upon musical sounds. By learning to precisely tune your instrument, you not only insure a true pitch in performance, but also greatly improved yourself as a musician.

An essential device for the beginning student is a guitar tuner. Inexpensive and readily available at any music store, the tuner instantly shows that a string is sharp or flat and allows you to adjust the instrument until the needle indicates that the string is in tune. Eventually, with the feedback of the tuner's needle, you will recognize the difference between sharp and flat and need the tuner less frequently.

The names of the strings are E (or 1st), B (or 2nd), G (or 3rd), D (or 4th), A (or 5th), and E (or 6th). The strings of the guitar are numbered according to their size: E (1st) is lightest, B (2nd) is slightly heavier, and so on, up to the E (6th) string, which is heaviest of all. When using a tuner, be sure that the name of the string you are tuning is properly indicated, otherwise, you might accidentally tune the 1st string to B instead of E. Have your teacher assist you until you are proficient at using the tuner.

Tuning to the CD

Tracks 45–50 of the included CD are tuning tracks. They provide the sound of the individual guitar strings, tuned to the reference pitch of A-440 (440 cycles per second). Match the pitch of each string with the pitch on the CD. This, and an A-440 tuner, will allow you to play in tune with the accompaniment tracks on the CD.

Tuning to a Piano

The six open strings of the guitar match the pitches of the piano keyboard as shown in figure 2. Observe that five of the strings are tuned below middle C of the piano. When tuning, the string should be loosened to a tone slightly below the desired pitch, then brought up to pitch. In this manner, all the slack is taken up in the gear mechanism of the tuning keys.

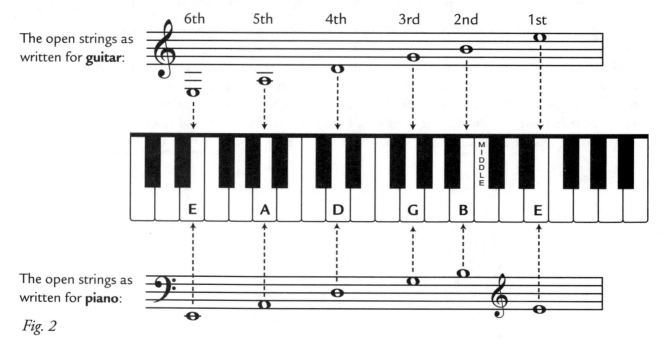

Fig. 2

Further necessary tuning cannot be accomplished unless the action of the guitar is well adjusted, as described in the previous section "The Playing Condition of a Guitar."

Tuning the Guitar to Itself

Another way to tune is to tune the guitar with itself, one string relative to the other, after a string has been tuned with the aid of another instrument. This approach requires you to readily recognize when a pitch is sharp or flat—a skill that is acquired with time. Figure 3 represents a section of the guitar fingerboard.

1. Place a finger on the E (6th) string, just back of the 5th fret, to obtain the correct pitch for the A string.

2. Place a finger on the A string, just back of the 5th fret, for the correct pitch of the D string.

3. Place a finger on the D string, just back of the 5th fret, for the pitch of the G string.

4. Place a finger on the G string, just back of the 4th fret (one fret lower than for other strings), for the pitch of the B string.

5. Place a finger on the B string, just back of the 5th fret, for the pitch of the E (1st) string.

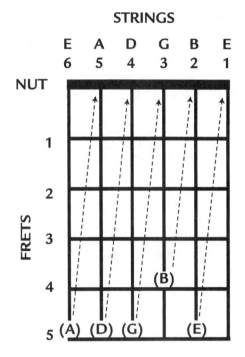

Fig. 3

After the guitar has been tuned as previously explained, you should always make a final test by playing the E major chord shown in figure 4.

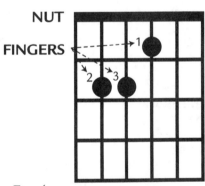

Fig. 4

With the left fingers in position for the E major chord, holding the three strings **firmly** against the frets, strum all six strings, beginning with the 6th. Use the right thumb, quite relaxed, to glide slowly from one string to the next until all are ringing clear. This is, without a doubt, one of the most beautiful major chords on the guitar when the instrument is in tune; it should have a thoroughly pleasant sound with absolutely no feeling of discord. With a little practice, you will be able to tell whether or not a particular string is out of tune merely by strumming the E major chord slowly and listening to each tone as it is sounded.

At first, the guitar tuner is essential for tuning your guitar. As you develop your tuning skills, you might only need the tuner to put the 6th string in tune and then use the "tune the guitar to itself" method to finish tuning the guitar. Either method of tuning the guitar is valid and useful depending on your knowledge of music and the instrument.

How Music Is Written

The Elements of Notation

1. Music is written on a *staff* consisting of five lines and four spaces that are numbered from the bottom upward (a), and on *ledger lines* and added spaces numbered outward from the staff (b):

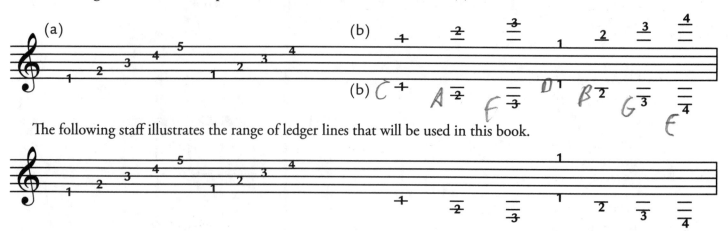

The following staff illustrates the range of ledger lines that will be used in this book.

2. The first seven letters of the alphabet (A B C D E F G) are used to name notes in music. The *treble clef* or *G clef* sign is placed on the staff so that the scroll encloses the second line, establishing the position of the note G.

3. Five kinds of notes and their equivalent rests appear in this book: whole notes, half notes, quarter notes, eighth notes, and sixteenth notes. The stems of consecutive eighth or sixteenth notes are usually joined with *beams* instead of being written separately.

Values of Notes and Rests

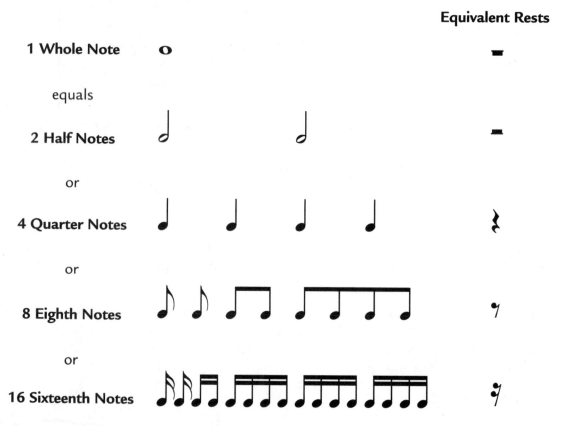

5/13 pause 4 beats
" 2 "

Eminor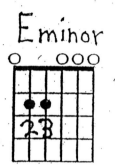

Aminor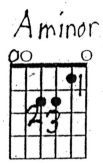

Dminor

Aminor⁷

C⁷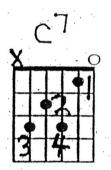

Eminor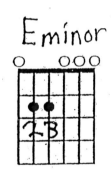

B⁷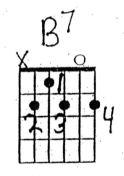

Eminor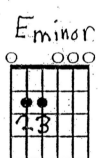

4. A *measure* (a) is a division of time by which the movement of music and its rhythm is regulated. The staff is divided into measures by vertical lines called *bar lines* (b).

5. The *time signature* is a combination of numbers set just after the clef sign. The following definition is important to remember:

> The top figure shows the number of counts in each measure.
> The bottom figure shows the kind of note that receives one count.

"Four-Four" Time or Common Time

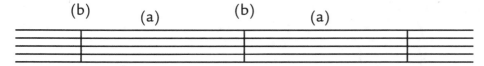

four counts to a measure
a quarter note receives one count

Count: 1   2   3   4   1   2   3   4   1   2   3   4   1   2   3   4   1   2   3   4

"Six-Eight" Time

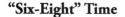

six counts to a measure
an eighth note receives one count

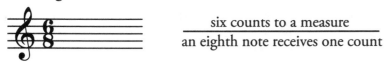

Count: 1   2   3   4   5   6   1   2   3   4   5   6   1   2   3   4   5   6

Other commonly used time signatures are ¾, 2/4, and 3/8.

6. The *double bar* (a) marks the end of a section, movement, or composition. A *dotted double bar* (b) means to repeat from the preceding dotted double bar (c). If there is no dotted double bar preceding the section (d), repeat the composition from its beginning.

Important note to beginning students: The *Guitar Note Speller* was written by Aaron Shearer as a companion volume to *Classic Guitar Technique*. Learning to read music on the guitar is unquestionably easier and more thorough when a writing book is used.

Holding the Guitar

Since the first publication of this book in 1959, many devices have been developed to assist the guitarist in supporting the guitar. From the adjustable footstand and the thigh pad to the A-frame and the Shearer Classic Guitar Strap, all contribute towards more comfortably supporting the guitar in various ways. It is not the intention of this book to recommend which system is best, for this is a personal decision; rather, the recommendation here is that each student should proceed with an attitude of experimentation and work closely with an experienced teacher to find the most advantageous manner for holding the guitar.

The Footstand

The footstand was the device originally used in this book and is still popular.

1. Place the footstand on the floor about six inches in front of the front left chair leg so that it is aligned with the front left and right rear chair legs. Generally, the height of the footstand can vary from four to eight inches or even higher, if necessary, according to your physique. Notice that the higher the footstand is, the more flexed your knee becomes, which will lead to discomfort over long periods of time.

2. Sit on the forward part of the chair, and place the left foot on the footstand so that the left foot and leg line up with the left front and right rear chair legs, as illustrated in figure 7. To do this properly, you should sit forward and slightly to the left. Sitting in this manner allows you to drop the thigh down to support the guitar. Also, be sure your back is properly aligned and that you are not leaning to one side or the other.

3. Place the waist of the guitar snugly over the left thigh. Lower the right thigh so that it is supported by the ball of the foot. Move the left leg to the right to cradle the guitar between the thighs.

4. Adjust the height of the footstand to position the guitar so that the head is approximately at eye level. The forearm rests on the upper bout of the guitar with the fingers and thumb placed on the strings as shown in figures 5 and 6.

Fig. 5   *Fig. 6*

5. Lean forward slightly so that the upper edge of the guitar rests against your chest, keeping the shoulders relaxed and on an even horizontal plane, and with the torso turned slightly toward the left knee.

6. Tilt the guitar slightly outward to allow the right forearm to pass more easily over the upper bout. This will improve the visibility of all six strings while permitting the back soundboard to vibrate more freely.

Figure 7 shows the correct position for holding the guitar when using a footstand.

1. Vertical axis passes through footstand, thigh, and diagonal legs of chair.

2. Guitar is placed somewhat under right arm and shoulder.

3. Head of the guitar is forward.

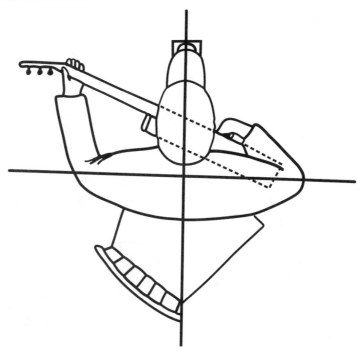

Fig. 7

It's important to remember that your goal is to have full access to the strings and fingerboard without sacrificing the alignment of your shoulders or back. With this in mind, experiment with adjusting the guitar in relation to your body. This will help you learn how your body should approach the guitar to best support your hand's access.

The following are some parameters for adjustment:

1. Moving the head of the guitar forward and back.

2. Moving the head of the guitar up and down.

3. Tilting the guitar outward and inward.

4. Changing the overall height of the guitar.

5. Changing the overall left/right relationship of the guitar to your body.

You should always be sensitive to your seating position. As you progress and evolve as a musician, so will your seating position. Perhaps the footstand is just a starting point; though it is the traditional way of supporting the instrument, it is not the only way. The following are some alternatives that better assist the musician in maintaining alignment and full access to the instrument.

The A-Frame

The main purpose of the A-frame's development was to elevate the guitar without uncomfortably elevating the thigh. Attaching to the guitar with four suction cups, it enables the guitarist to sit with both feet on the floor if the chair is low enough, or can be combined with the footstand to achieve a more elevated position if the chair is higher. Unfortunately, the A-frame does not allow the instrument to be moved far enough to the guitarist's right to allow maximum leverage in the left hand.

Fig. 8   *Fig. 9*

The Shearer Classic Guitar Strap

Perhaps one of the most innovative and practical means of supporting the guitar is the Shearer Classic Guitar Strap (found at most music stores or on the web at www.aaronshearer.com). This device, along with the accompanying handbook, assists you in finding a comfortable position for sitting as well as standing. As stated earlier, the primary goal in the seated position is to have full access to the instrument with both hands while maintaining muscular alignment. The Shearer Classic Guitar Strap achieves this by positioning the instrument higher and to the right of the torso. The placement of the strap creates a tilt to the instrument so that the right arm can easily pass over the upper bout. This will also create positioning that provides a view of all six strings, while permitting the back soundboard to vibrate freely. Attached to the guitar with Velcro®, it provides a secure method of supporting the guitar in a position that achieves muscular alignment of the back, maximum leverage for the left hand, and full access to the instrument for both hands.

Fig. 10

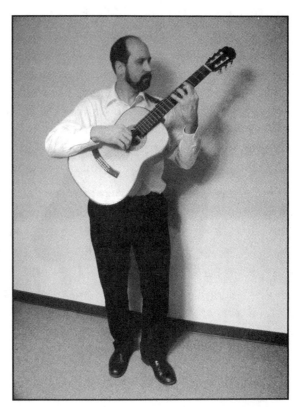

Fig. 11

In any case, an attitude of experimentation and willingness to proceed with an open mind should always be maintained. Work closely with your teacher, and practice in front of a mirror so you have some visual feedback as to whether you are leaning towards the left hand, thus causing muscular misalignment, or playing with the instrument too low, thus not achieving maximum leverage in the hands.

As previously mentioned, as you develop as a musician, so will your seating position. You might notice that certain movements are not feasible in your current position, and with slight adjustments of moving the guitar up and to the right, greater ease of access can be achieved.

The Right Hand

This section of *Classic Guitar Technique* is extremely important. The thumb and fingers of the right hand are responsible for sounding the strings with accuracy and speed, and for producing different shades of tone with varying degrees of volume.

Be aware that the process of playing any musical instrument is not entirely natural for the muscles involved. This is especially true concerning the right hand in playing the guitar, so we must operate within the parameters of how our hands were designed to work. First, the right hand must be placed in a position that ultimately brings the desired results of utmost accuracy, speed, and control of tone and volume while following basic concepts of positive muscular activity (soon explained under "Placing the Right Hand" on page 21. Once these concepts are understood, the student must carefully reinforce them so that positive habits of movement will be created.

There is never a situation in guitar playing where pain should be present. Pain is your body's way of saying that a habit you are executing is damaging. Tired muscles are one thing, but pain and tingling in the arms and hands is quite another.

Realize that any new movement is going to feel unusual at first. Though your present positioning and movement may feel natural to you, it may not be the most positive movement habit. Take the time with a mirror to analyze how you are moving in relation to the guidelines in this book. Be patient, and only reinforce the desired habit. If you see your old habit reemerging in the mirror, then stop, correct the position or movement, and start again. It's important to make these changes with remedial exercises or material, and it is usually necessary to avoid repertoire where the old habit is prevalent. Continue to ask yourself the question, "Is this the habit that I want to reinforce as part of my playing?"

The nails of the right hand are what help produce the beautiful tone associated with the classic guitar. In the beginning, your nails will be short and unable to strike the string. Allow your nails to grow, and continually contour them to the "basic" shape as outlined in "Initial Care of the Right Hand Nails" on page 24. As soon as you are able to contact the string with your nails, follow the instructions outlined in "Care and Use of the Right Hand Nails" on page 50.

Again, be patient; new habits of movement are not instantly developed, but take time to be formed. Initially, a new habit cannot be felt, but must be seen; work in front of a mirror so that you can see the position and movement you are creating. Keep exercises simple so you can focus on the new positive habit and avoid selections that allow you to "slip" back into old habits of motion or position.

Names of the Right Hand Fingers

In guitar music, the customary indications for the thumb and
fingers of the right hand are from Latin designations:

> p = pollex
> i = index
> m = medius
> a = annularis
> ~~c = chico~~

The little finger of the right hand (c) is generally not used to
pluck the strings. If properly relaxed, it will naturally follow the
movements of a.

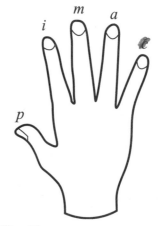

Fig. 12

Placing the Right Hand

1. Place the right forearm on the upper bout of the guitar
   as shown in figure 13. Be sure the guitar contacts the
   arm below the elbow, creating a pivot point, or *fulcrum*,
   for the arm.

Fig. 13

Do not allow the guitar to fall into the crook of the
arm as in figure 14.

Fig. 14

2. Viewed from the top, the wrist must be kept in alignment for the arm's muscles to pull in a straight line (fig. 15).

Fig. 15

Do not allow the arm to deviate or curve off to one side or the other (figs. 16 & 17).

Fig. 16

Fig. 17

3. Viewed from the side, the wrist should assume a slight arch (fig. 18).

Fig. 18

The wrist should not be flexed to create a high arch (fig. 19) or extended to the point of creating a collapsed arch (fig. 20).

Fig. 19

Fig. 20

4. Beginning students may wish to rest the thumb on a string to assist in hand support and stability (fig. 21).

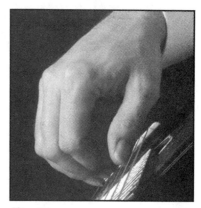

Fig. 21

Eventually, you will assume a position with the thumb hanging downward, not touching the strings (fig. 22).

Fig. 22

5. The hand is tilted to the left so that, when viewed from the front or back, *a* is perpendicular to the top of the guitar while *i* and *m* create an angle of fewer than 90 degrees to the top of the guitar. This will also allow the thumb to move up the string with greater area for its follow-through (fig. 23).

Fig. 23

6. Be sure your shoulders stay horizontal and relaxed. Try not to hold tension in the shoulders—frequently remind yourself to relax and let the tension in your shoulders go.

Be sure to continue to work in front of a mirror so that proper placement is easily recognized. If the images in your mirror do not look like the pictures found here, then stop, make adjustments, and continue to reinforce the habit of proper placement. Seating position and right hand placement should frequently be the focus of your practice. Even the accomplished player should revisit these issues so that bad habits are not formed. Continually check and adjust your position to reinforce the positive habits you want to form.

Rest Stroke and Free Stroke

You will use two types of right hand finger strokes when playing the classic guitar: the *rest stroke*, often referred to by its Spanish name, *apoyando*, and the *free stroke*, also known as *tirando*. The rest stroke occurs when, after playing a string, the finger comes to rest against the adjacent lower string. The free stroke occurs when, after playing a string, the finger passes freely over the adjacent lower string.

To begin your study, we will first work with the fingers in rest stroke and then proceed to working with the thumb in free stroke. Ultimately, this combination will enable us to play music in two parts: a bass line with the thumb, and a melodic line with the fingers.

Initial Care of the Right Hand Nails

The beautiful tone that is produced from the classic guitar is created from the use of nails on the player's right hand. In the beginning, you may not have nails on the right hand that are long enough to adequately contact the string, let alone produce a tone. At this point, you want to allow the nails of your right hand to begin to grow out. With the use of a diamond-type file found at any drug store, shape the nail so that it has a smooth, gentle curve absent of any ragged edges. This will produce a foundation for you to begin growing a nail to a proper length and contoured as described in the section "Care and Use of the Right Hand Nails" on page 50.

Until you are able to use your right hand nails, be sure that the string contacts your finger as close to the nail as possible. This will create a habit that discourages you from allowing the finger to contact too deeply into the strings.

Care of the Left Hand Nails

The left hand nails should be clipped short so that the nails do not contact the frets or fretboard when you push down or stop the strings. A pair of nail clippers will do an adequate job of keeping your left hand nails short so that proper technique can be acquired.

Rest Stroke Movement of the Right Hand Fingers

1. With the right hand set up as previously mentioned in "Positioning the Right Hand," prepare the thumb on the 4th string as shown in figure 24.

Fig. 24

2. Place *i* on the 1st string as seen in figure 25, so that the string is placed between the flesh and nail. If you presently have no nail, then place the string as close to the end of the finger as possible.

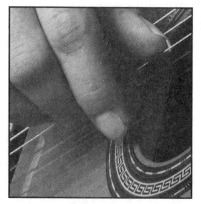

Fig. 25

3. After playing the string, the finger will come to rest on the adjacent B string. (fig. 26).

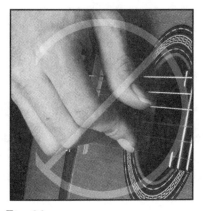

Fig. 26

4. Be sure to keep your tip joint firm (fig. 27) so that it does not collapse (fig. 28).

Fig. 27

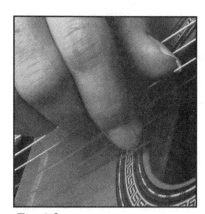

Fig. 28

5. Once you feel comfortable with *i*, proceed to practicing this movement with *m* and then *a*.

6. When playing *a*, be sure that *c* moves along with *a*. Do not hold it still or allow it to stick out, for this will form bad habits of tension.

Recommended Procedure for Practice

Before attempting to play any exercise, it is important to be sure you understand what notes you are about to play and where they are on the guitar. A simple, good habit to form is to say the notes out loud and clarify in your mind's eye where each is located on the instrument. For example, to prepare for exercise 1, once you clarify that E, B, and G are the 1st, 2nd, and 3rd open strings, respectively, set the guitar down and do the following exercise:

1. Work in small segments, perhaps a few measures at a time.

2. As you say the note out loud, visualize your finger playing that string. This will not only reinforce the note names, but will also clarify which string is which.

3. Be sure to say the names in the proper rhythm so that timing is also reinforced.

4. As you say the notes out loud and visualize their locations, move your fingers as if you are playing the guitar. Once again, reinforce the proper motion of the fingers and their timing. This process is called *prereading*.

5. Once you feel comfortable, proceed to play the segment on the guitar, but continue to say the note names out loud and clarify in your mind's eye the location of each note on the guitar as you play it. We call this step *say and play*.

6. Proceed slowly to minimize errors and feel confident about what you are doing. Once you have successfully completed this with the first segment, continue on to the next segment and repeat the process.

7. Finally, visualize and recite the two segments together, and then play them.

8. Continue in this manner until the exercise is completed.

9. If you have difficulty with a specific segment or measure, isolate it, and repeatedly preread, and say and play, the problematic area. This is called *isolating*, or practicing an *isolation*. The TNT software on the accompanying CD allows you to loop any specific section and work on it as an isolation.

Not only will this process reinforce the name and location of each note, it will also develop the most important concept of playing: concentration. By training your mind to focus on the information, you will develop powerful habits of maintaining concentration while performing more complex tasks.

Stopping the Strings at the End of a Piece

CD tracks 1–14 have an audible "stop" at the end of each selection. This is to help you develop the positive habit of stopping the vibration of the strings at the end of a piece. An effective and professional-looking way to do this is to turn your right hand from the wrist and place the flat left side against all six strings as illustrated in figure 29.

Fig. 29

The Open 1st, 2nd, and 3rd Strings

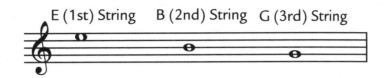

E (1st) String   B (2nd) String   G (3rd) String

Now that we understand how to use the fingers in rest stroke, we can apply this knowledge to play the first three open strings. With your thumb prepared on the 5th string, group your fingers on the first three open strings. For now, *i* will play the 3rd string (G), *m* will play the 2nd string (B), and *a* will play the 1st string (E).

Be sure to begin by visualizing while saying the notes out loud or prereading. Clarify in your mind the location of each note on the guitar and which right hand finger you are going to use. Then say and play.

Exercise 1   **CD TRACK 1**
Be sure to preread, then say and play. Also, isolate any difficult sections.

Exercise 2   **CD TRACK 2**
Work slowly and evenly.

Exercise 3   **CD TRACK 3**

Exercise 4   **CD TRACK 4**
What is meant by $\frac{3}{4}$? (See page 15.)

Movement of the Right Hand Thumb

The right hand thumb is generally used for playing bass notes on the classic guitar. To begin developing movement of the right hand thumb, you will perform an exercise to reinforce the basic necessary motion.

1. Away from the guitar, place your right hand on the back of your left hand, assuming a position similar to how it approaches the strings (fig. 30).

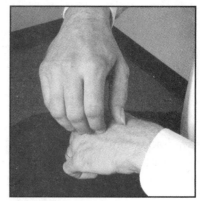

Fig. 30

2. Extend the thumb from the wrist joint, and be sure that the tip joint does not also extend. Movement is entirely from the wrist joint, while the middle and tip joints are kept relaxed (fig. 31).

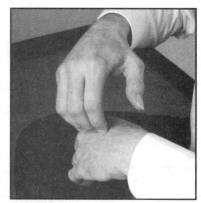

Fig. 31

3. Close the wrist joint until the thumb comes to rest against *i* at the tip joint (fig. 32).

4. Repeat this exercise, extending and flexing *p* at the wrist joint. Frequently practice it to reinforce the basic motion that will be used for free stroke thumb motion.

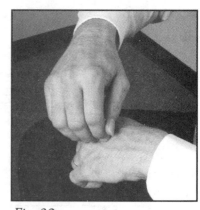

Fig. 32

Free Stroke with the Thumb

1. With the right hand set up as previously mentioned in "Placing the Right Hand" (page 21), prepare the fingers on the strings with *i* on the 3rd string, *m* on the 2nd string, and *a* on the 1st string. The left tips of the fingers will be in contact with the strings (fig. 33).

2. Place the thumb on the 4th string with the string contacting the left side of the nail, as shown in figure 33. If your nail has not yet developed, place the string as close to the tip as possible.

3. Move the thumb from the wrist joint in the same manner that has been practiced; be sure to keep the tip joint firm so that it does not collapse.

Fig. 33

4. Play the 4th string and allow the thumb to come to rest against the tip joint of *i* (fig.34).

Fig. 34

5. Repeat this motion by preparing the finger on the 4th string before playing it. Practice this until the motion becomes familiar.

6. When you feel comfortable with the 4th string, proceed to playing the 5th string (figs. 35 & 36) and then the 6th string (figs. 37 & 38) with the thumb. Notice a greater amount of extension is required from the thumb to reach the lower pitched strings. Also notice that, as you play the 5th and 6th strings, the thumb will pass freely over the 4th string when playing the 5th, and over the 4th and 5th strings when playing the 6th (figs. 35–38).

Fig. 35

Fig. 36

Fig. 37

Fig. 38

The Open 4th, 5th, and 6th Strings

Now that you understand how your thumb should move to play the string and how to approach an exercise, we will apply this to learning the open bass notes.

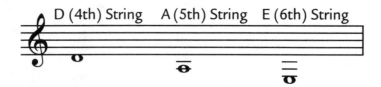

Exercise 5 is played entirely with *p* executing the free stroke as described in "Free Stroke with the Thumb" on page 28.

1. First, count each beat out loud in accordance with the time signature (see page 15).

2. Away from the guitar, and working in small segments, preread by saying each note out loud in rhythm while visualizing the location of the thumb playing the appropriate string. Move your hands in the air as if playing the string while naming it out loud in rhythm. (See "Recommended Procedure for Practice" on page 26.)

3. When you are comfortable with the segment, say and play it on the guitar. Choose a slow tempo so that you feel comfortable and not rushed. Try to minimize confusion and errors. If you are making mistakes, you are going too fast.

Exercise 5   CD TRACK 5
Play slowly and without confusion or error!

The Dotted Half Note

A dot placed after a note increases the time value of that note by
one half. For example, the *dotted half note* sounds for three full counts:

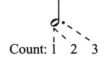

Count: 1　2　3

Each measure of exercise 6 has three counts, and the quarter note receives one count.

Exercise 6　CD TRACK 6
Play with *p* in free stroke.

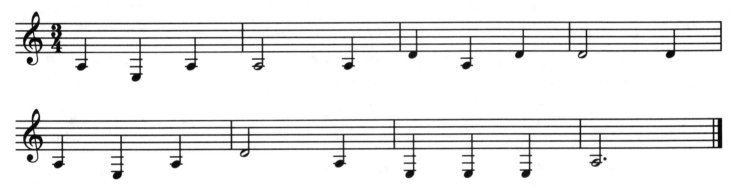

Exercise 7　CD TRACK 7

Exercise 8　CD TRACK 8

Combining Thumb and Fingers

The following exercises use the fingers and thumb together. This will be the foundation for what will eventually become music in two parts (*melody* and *bass*).

Notice in exercise 9 that the fingers will play the treble strings (E, B, and G) while the thumb will play the bass strings (D, A, and E).

Before you proceed, remember to work first with a small segment, which you will preread and visualize while reciting the notes and mentally locating them on the guitar. Try the exercise by saying the right hand fingers while clarifying their location on the guitar. Continue by playing and saying out loud.

Exercise 9
Play slowly and carefully. Isolate any problematic sections.

Exercise 10

go to p. 37

Alternation

Once you feel comfortable playing the treble strings with the fingers as in exercises 1–4, you are ready to play strings with alternating fingers. Especially when playing a selection that requires speed and fluency, it is impractical to keep repeating the same finger. Alternating fingers *i* and *m*, or the slightly more difficult *m* and *a*, is how single lines and scales will be played fluently and smoothly.

Let's begin alternating:

1. With the right hand set up as previously mentioned in "Placing the Right Hand," prepare the thumb on the 4th string as seen in figure 39.

Fig. 39

2. Place *i* on the 2nd string as seen in figure 40, so that the string is placed between the flesh and nail. If you presently have no nail, then place the string as close to the end of the finger as possible. Be sure to keep your tip joint firm so that it does not collapse.

Fig. 40

3. After playing the string, *i* will come to rest on the adjacent G string (fig. 41).

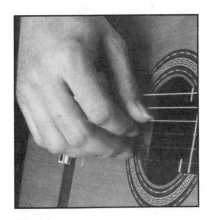

Fig. 41

4. As the B string is being played with *i*, extend *m* and prepare it on the B string so that it is ready to play the next stroke (fig. 42).

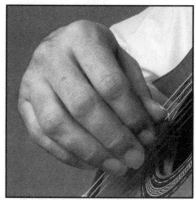

Fig. 42

5. Now play the B string with *m*, and as *m* plays the string, *i* will extend and prepare on the B string (fig. 43).

Fig. 43

6. The important point to remember is that alternation occurs when the fingers are moving equal and opposite. When *i* is flexed and resting on an adjacent string, *m* is out preparing to play, and when *m* is flexed and resting on an adjacent string, *i* is out preparing to play.

When beginning to learn alternation, it is easier to prepare each finger on the string. Though this tends to mute the string and make your playing choppy, or *staccato*, it will promote security and reinforce the habit of proper finger placement on the string. As you become secure with the concept of alternation, you will find the pause of preparation so brief that the notes will become smooth, or *legato*. This will bring a continuity to your stroke and sound. The perceptive student will notice that, prior to playing a string, the finger will pause over the string and allow it to ring until the exact moment the finger strikes with the same firm contact as the prepared stroke.

Exercises for Alternation

The following exercises will look familiar. They are repeated here so that you can more freely focus on alternating *i* and *m* rather than concerning yourself as much with what note comes next. They are now fingered for alternation and more frequently so you can make sure you are truly alternating and not repeating fingers. Though they may seem obvious, get into the habit now of writing in your right hand fingerings. Complete the right hand fingerings for the following exercises.

Exercise 11 CD TRACK 9

Proceed **slowly** and be sure you are **alternating**! Say the right hand fingerings out loud.

* When playing with fingers in alternation, it is necessary to shift the right hand when changing strings using a technique called *string crossing*. (See page 40.)

Exercise 12 CD TRACK 10

Play **slowly** and **evenly**, with careful alternation of fingers! Isolate difficult sections.

Exercise 13 CD TRACK 11

Exercise 14 CD TRACK 12

After practicing exercises 11–14 with *i* and *m*, try them with *m* and *a*. Be sure to alternate, and when *m* moves, *i* will follow along, just as when *a* moves, *c* will follow along. **Make sure that *c* does not stick out!**

The Left Hand

Identifying the Left Hand Fingers

The customary designations in guitar music for the fingers of the left hand are as follows:

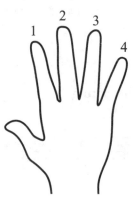

        index finger = 1
        middle finger = 2
        ring finger = 3
        pinky = 4

Fig. 44

Once you feel comfortable with the open string exercises, begin to practice while *stopping* (pressing down on) a string. Be sure the nails of the left hand are clipped back so that they do not touch the fingerboard or fret.

Notice the following points while viewing the left hand positions in figures 45 and 46:

1. Strings must always be held firmly against the frets to produce a good, clear tone.

2. Each finger should curve so that only the tip rests precisely upon the string, **just in back of the fret.**

3. Position the hand so the fingers are perpendicular to the fretboard.

4. Make sure the guitar head is up high enough so that the wrist does not have to bend excessively.

5. Once a finger is placed, never lift it until necessary to play a lower note or a note on another string.

6. Fingers must never lift far from the fingerboard; keep them hovering closely over the strings.

7. The thumb should always remain on the neck as shown in figure 46. Maintain a position approximately opposite the point between the 1st and 2nd fingers. Never should the thumb protrude over the edge of the fingerboard on the bass side.

Fig. 45

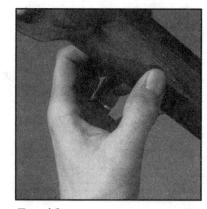

Fig. 46

Notes on the E, or 1st, String

E — open
F — 1st fret / 1st finger
G — 3rd fret / 3rd finger

* Numbers next to notes indicate which left hand fingers to use.
A circle indicates an open (non-fingered) string.

E

F

G

Continue to reinforce the habit of following the "Recommended Procedure for Practice" on page 26. Now you will mark your left hand fingerings in the music and say them when prereading or saying and playing. Doing so clarifies the following information:

- Name of the note
- Location of the note on the guitar (string and fret)
- Left hand finger
- Right hand finger

12/7

Exercise 15 CD TRACK 13

1. Play **slowly**, first with *i* and *m* in rest stroke, then with *m* and *a*.
2. X = hold. Do not lift the finger until necessary!
3. Write in the fingerings for the left hand and right hand.

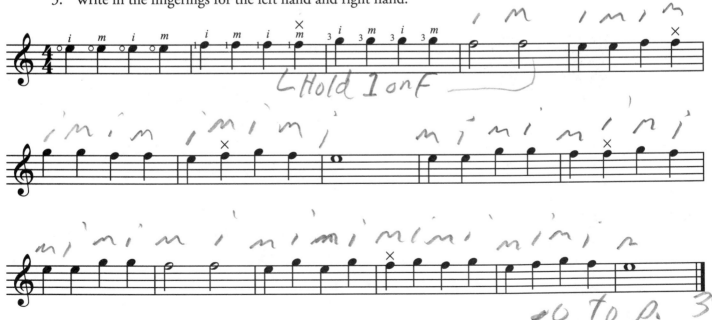

go to p. 39

Exercise 16 CD TRACK 14

Close examination of your **finger action** is recommended:

1. Tip joints should be firm, neither rigid nor collapsing.

2. Fingers should lift only high enough to make the next stroke.

3. Right hand remains steady; only fingers move to make the strokes.

Notes on the B, or 2nd, String

B   C   D

open   1st fret   3rd fret
          1st finger   3rd finger

B   C   D

Exercise 17   **CD TRACK 15**

Use rest stroke with *i* and *m*, then *m* and *a*.

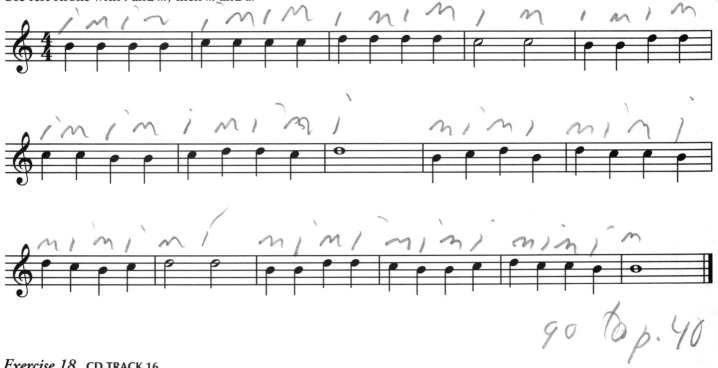

Exercise 18   **CD TRACK 16**

String Crossing

When notes are played on different strings with alternating fingers, it is necessary to shift the right hand when changing strings. This is called *string crossing*, and is illustrated in measure 4 of exercise 19, where you must shift to the 1st string to play E after playing D on the 2nd string. This shift is performed from the elbow, which opens slightly to allow the hand to shift towards the 1st string. While doing this, avoid the tendency to open the hand or collapse the wrist to reach for the next-higher-pitched string. The shift is simply created by opening the elbow when playing a higher string, such as the 1st string, or closing the elbow when playing a lower string, such as the 2nd string. Figures 92 and 93 on page 80 illustrate the elbow closed while playing the 6th string and open while playing the 1st string.

Review exercises 15, 16, 17, and 18 before playing exercise 19.

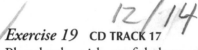

Exercise 19 **CD TRACK 17**

Play slowly, with careful alternation, first with *i* and *m*, then with *m* and *a*.
Be sure the elbow opens and closes during string crossing!

go to p. 43

Music in Two Parts: Alternation of Fingers with the Thumb in the Bass

The solo guitar of "Prelude No. 1" consists of two parts: the *treble* (melody) and *bass*. Exercise 20 is just the melody, and exercise 21, which employs the *tie*, is the bass. Thoroughly study each exercise separately, and then play them together as "Prelude No. 1," your first solo.

Exercise 20 (Treble part of "Prelude No. 1")

The Tie

A curved line joining two notes of the same pitch is called a *tie*:

A tie indicates that the second note is a continuation of the first note and is held for its duration without being struck. It is counted with the usual number of beats, but simply not sounded again.

Exercise 21 (Bass part of "Prelude No. 1")

Before proceeding to "Prelude No. 1," a careful review of exercises 9, 10, 20, and 21 is recommended until the following are achieved:

1. You are thoroughly familiar with all the notes.

2. You can maintain an **even rhythm,** at least slowly (♩ = 72).

3. The tip segments of the right fingers are **firm** while **strict alternation** is maintained.

4. The right thumb (*p*) executes **free stroke** with reasonable accuracy, and the **hand is steady.**

Realize that the fingers will continue to alternate while the thumb plays the bass. Practice this movement form until it is familiar and comfortable.

"Prelude No. 1" has a duet part (Gtr. II), which may be played by a second guitarist or from the CD. The first guitar (Gtr. I) is the solo part. You must be comfortable playing "Prelude No. 1" as a solo before attempting to play the duet along with CD track 18.

Prelude No. 1   **CD TRACK 18**

Exercise 22   **CD TRACK 19**

Exercise 22 begins on the last beat of the measure. Begin counting with "4, 1–2–3–4, 1–2–3–4," etc.
First alternate *i* and *m*, then *m* and *a*.

Rest on beat 4.

Practice the treble and bass parts in the solo (guitar I) of "Prelude No. 2" separately, then together. The quarter rest on the first beat of measure 5 indicates that the preceding bass note may be stopped with *p*. At this time, however, it is recommended that you permit the bass to sound without regard to the rests; no offensive harmony will occur in this piece, and it is not necessary to develop the technique of stopping bass notes now. When you feel comfortable with "Prelude No. 2" as a solo, play along with CD track 20 and enjoy it as a duet.

Prelude No. 2 **CD TRACK 20**

You should make a continuous effort to think of where the notes are located on the guitar, and then find them without looking at the instrument. **The eyes should be kept on the music!**

For the fastest, easiest progress, you are urged to apply the visualization steps outlined on page 26. After you are comfortable with "Prelude No. 3," proceed to play it as a duet with CD track 21.

Prelude No. 3 **CD TRACK 21**

Quiz this or p.48

Prelude No. 4 CD TRACK 22

go to p.48

Notes on the G, or 3rd, String

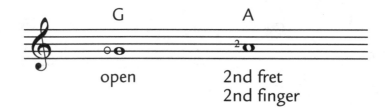

G

A

Always apply the "Recommended Procedure for Practice" on page 26 when beginning to study new material.

Exercise 23 CD TRACK 23

Preread, then say and play. Work slowly, with control and accuracy. Alternate first with *i* and *m*, then *m* and *a*.

Prelude No. 5 **CD TRACK 24**
Keep the **right hand steady!** Use movements from thumb and fingers **only**.

Etude No. 1 **CD TRACK 25**

Prelude No. 6 CD TRACK 26

Care and Use of the Right Hand Nails

The world's finest and most widely recognized classic guitarists use their fingernails in conjunction with the fleshy part of their fingertips to sound the strings of the guitar. For a variety of reasons, some students are unable to keep their nails in good playing condition, but they should not be discouraged in their efforts to play the guitar, as much pleasure may be obtained from playing the instrument well without nails. However, the serious and aspiring student of the classic guitar **must** consider the use of the nails to be absolutely necessary. Without the nails, execution and volume lack brilliance; and, most important, the tonal resources of the guitar, to a great extent, remain dormant.

Students who have developed proper control of the firmness of their tip joints will have little difficulty using the nails. The strings should be struck with the nail while the fleshy part of the fingertip contacts at the initial placement to produce a firm contact as previously described in detail. When the nails have grown to proper length, they will automatically sound the strings as each stroke is executed.

No attempt will be made here to set down definite or precise rules regarding the shape of the nails, because their characteristics vary with the individual. By studying figures 47–50, you will acquire some knowledge as to how different types of fingernails are shaped; then, through practice, you will soon learn how to shape your own for best results.

Keep the following important points in mind:

1. With the right hand in correct playing position (as described on page 21), only the left tip of the nail will strike the strings.

2. Nails must not be too long; no more than 1/16 inch of the nails should strike the strings.

3. Nails should be shaped by holding a fine diamond-type file or emery board underneath at an angle (figs. 47 & 48), forming a flat or straight surface for striking the strings.

Fig. 47

Fig. 48

4. Nails that tend to grow in a hook or curve will assume an angled shape (fig. 49); those which are straight will become rounded (fig. 50).

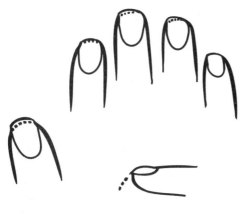

Fig. 49

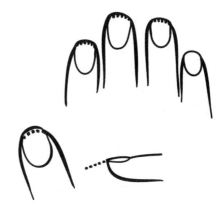

Fig. 50

5. After shaping from underneath, lightly smooth any rough top edges.

6. As required, in accordance with the texture of the nails, the striking edges may finally be polished with very fine emery cloth, 600-grit sandpaper, or equivalent.

7. Keep the tip segment of each finger firm, but controlled, so the correctly shaped nail will glide freely across the string. If there is a sensation of "hooking" or "catching" during the stroke, the nail has not been properly flattened from underneath or is too long, or the tip segment of the finger is too firm. Be sure not to let the tip segments collapse when playing.

8. **Most important!** *Listen to the tone;* if it is harsh or unpleasing to the ear in some respect, alter the shape of the nails slightly. Experiment until you obtain a beautiful tone; this is a prime essential for the concert guitarist.

Half Steps and Whole Steps

A *half step* is the distance from one note to the next nearest note, up or down, such as an open string to the 1st fret, or any fret to the next higher or lower fret.

A *whole step* consists of two half steps:

Chromatic Signs (Accidentals)

A *chromatic sign* raises or lowers a note one half step. A chromatic sign next to a note is called an *accidental*.

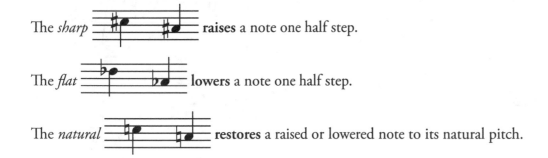

The *sharp* **raises** a note one half step.

The *flat* **lowers** a note one half step.

The *natural* **restores** a raised or lowered note to its natural pitch.

Notes on the E (1st) String
Open and First Four Frets
(Numbers indicate both fingers and frets.)

Notes on the B (2nd) String
Open and First Four Frets
(Numbers indicate both fingers and frets.)

When playing the above examples, you will quickly observe that some notes are identical in sound but have two names, such as F♯ and G♭, or C♯ and D♭. In fact, any note that has a sharp name also has a flat name, and vice versa.

Exercise 24

This *chromatic scale* exercise should be played 10 or more times at the very beginning of each practice session. Play **evenly**, with left fingers curved (see fig. 45, p. 36). Be sure to alternate with *i* and *m*, then *m* and *a*, and string cross from the elbow.

When ascending on any scale, the left fingers must remain down until changing to the next-higher string. **Never lift or place a finger until necessary.**

The Eighth Note

An eighth note ♪ or rest ⁊ receives one-half the time value of a quarter note.

In instrumental music, the stems of consecutive eighth notes are usually beamed together ♫♫ instead of each appearing with a flag ♪♪♪♪.

COUNT: 1   &   2   3   &   4   1   &   2   &   3   &   4   &   1   &   2   &   3   4   &

Music notation for the guitar is not always written as it sounds; sometimes it is notated for convenience in reading and writing. "Prelude No. 7" introduces an example of this type of notation. Each quarter note in the melody (treble part) also has a stem pointing downward to take the place of an eighth note in the accompaniment (bass part). When playing the bass notes, observe that each eighth note will actually sound for the duration of a quarter note.

When sounding the G string so that *i* comes to rest on the adjacent D string, the finger must be permitted to bounce outward to allow *p* to sound the D string immediately thereafter. See measures 2, 4, 6, 8, and 10.

Prelude No. 7
Play **slowly** and **evenly**.

COUNT: 1   &   2   &   3   &   4   &   1   &   etc.

How you practice is the most important factor in your study of music and the guitar. *Thoughtful* practice habits, applied regularly each day and with enough time, will assure you of success. Cultivate the enjoyment of knowing you are correctly learning to play one of the most beautiful and personal of instruments.

Free Stroke with the Fingers

The term *free stroke* means that the finger, in making its stroke, does not come to rest against the next adjacent string, but instead passes freely above it. Free stroke must be employed when tones of adjacent strings are required to ring, such as during arpeggios or in multi-voiced pieces.

In notation, rest stroke position is indicated with ▽, and free stroke position is indicated by ◡.

Placing the Hand for Free Stroke

1. Begin with the hand in position as if to play a rest stroke with *i* on the 1st string, and anchor *p* on the 5th string (fig. 51).

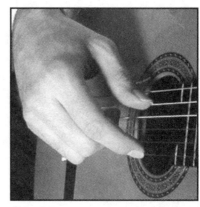

Fig. 51

2. Without moving the elbow, wrist, or hand, place the *i* fingertip on the 3rd string by flexing at the middle joint (fig. 52). Notice the finger is more flexed when in the free stroke position.

   Do not change the tilt of the hand or the alignment and arch of the wrist; the general position of the hand and arm remain the same. Only the degree of flex at the middle joint will change.

Fig. 52

3. As you play the string, keep your tip joints firm, and as your finger leaves the string, be sure it passes freely over the next-lower adjacent string (fig. 53).

Fig. 53

4. Notice the difference in finger placement and follow-through for the rest stroke (figs. 54 & 55) and free stroke (figs. 56 & 57).

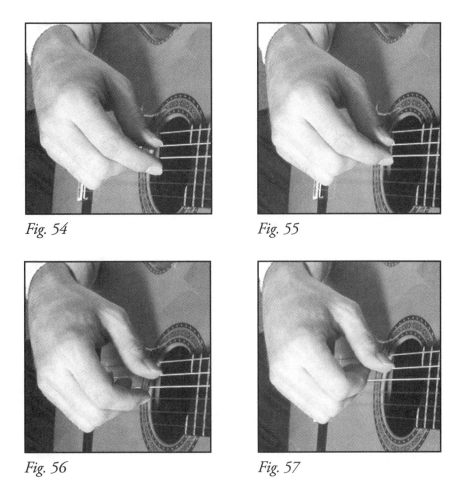

Fig. 54   Fig. 55

Fig. 56   Fig. 57

Exercise 25

Start this exercise using prepared free stroke just like you did when you started the rest stroke. For stability, you may anchor *p* on the 4th string as you play these exercises.

Begin **very slowly** and **carefully**! Exercise *i* alone, *m* alone, then *a* alone.

Important!

1. As you prepare to play, look in the mirror and make sure that your wrist is straight and not deviating, your arch is not collapsed, and your hand is tilted in.

2. As you play, be sure the finger passes freely over the next-lower adjacent string. The finger must execute a definite follow-through, down and into the palm, after sounding the string. It should **never** pop up and out, as that is very tension forming.

3. Keep your tip joints firm.

Take time now to do it correctly! Analyze each step thoughtfully, study specific problems, and practice slowly. Do not expect to perfect the free stroke movement in one or two sessions. It will generally become habit within a few weeks of good study. You will be richly rewarded for your patience in terms of tone, assurance, fluency, and volume.

Alternation with Fingers in Free Stroke

Now that the free stroke motion is being developed, you want to begin practicing free stroke alternation. This movement is similar to rest stroke alternation in that the fingers will move equal and opposite, but they are now in a free stroke position.

1. Place the hand in position for free stroke on the 1st string, with *p* anchored on the 4th string (fig. 58).

Fig. 58

2. As *i* plays the 1st string, *m* will extend to prepare its position for playing the 1st string (fig. 59). Notice that *a* and *c* will move along with *m* as *m* extends; **do not hold** *a* and *c* still or allow them to stick out.

Fig. 59

3. Once *m* has played, *i* will reset on the 1st string to prepare for its next stroke (fig. 60).

Fig. 60

4. Remember: alternation is equal and opposite. When *i* is playing, *m* is following through, and when *m* is playing, *i* is following through.

5. As with any new motion, you want to use a prepared stroke for each finger. This will cause a slight staccato sound at first that will diminish, and finally go away, as you acquire fluency.

As you practice exercises 26–30, be sure of the following:

1. Right hand is in its optimal position.

2. Fingers follow through towards the palm and are not allowed to pop up.

3. Fingers *m, a,* and *c* all move together when *m* is in motion.

4. Fingers *i* and *m* move equal and opposite during the motion.

Exercise 26

Exercise 27

Exercise 28

Exercise 29

Exercise 30
Remember to string cross from the elbow.

As you become comfortable using free stroke alternation with *i* and *m,* try exercises 26–30 using alternation with *m* and *a*. Realize that when *m* moves, *i* will move along with it, and *c* will move with *a* (figs. 61 & 62).

Fig. 61

Fig. 62

58

Free Stroke on Adjacent Strings

When a reasonable degree of relaxation and fluency have been attained with the foregoing exercises, thoroughly study exercises 31 and 32 **without the support of** p **resting on a string**. This is in preparation for exercises 33–36, in which free stroke movement with both the thumb and fingers is required. As you play these exercises, be sure the fingers truly alternate and that a and c move with m. Do not hold a and c stationary.

Exercise 31

Exercise 32

As you become comfortable using free stroke alternation with i and m, try exercises 31 and 32 using alternation with m and a. Realize that when m moves, i will move along with it, and c will move with a, as seen in figures 61 and 62.

Alternation Between the Thumb and Fingers

Exercises 33–36 will assist you in practicing alternation between p and the fingers. Be sure that all the fingers extend and flex together when playing. Do not hold any fingers stationary.

The problem requiring your most careful attention is that of holding the **right hand steady**, since all movement for each stroke comes from p or the fingers. You may find this increasingly difficult as p and the fingers become further separated. Keep the hand in position for the fingers to execute free stroke with maximum ease, then train p to extend as it reaches for lower strings. Do not lift the hand or cause it to bounce.

Practice exercises 33–36 also with p and m, and p and a.

Exercise 33   *Exercise 34*

Exercise 35

Exercise 36

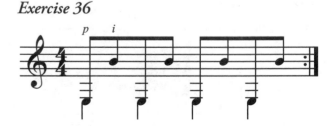

5/25 Quiz

Etude No. 2 **CD TRACK 27**

Execute with **all free strokes**. For now, do not attempt to stop the vibration of strings where rests appear.

go to p.68

Careful and continual review of the preceding material is advised until the right hand fingers and thumb move with a reasonable degree of accuracy and freedom. Progress will be faster if the fingers are properly trained from the beginning, so work slowly and carefully, and stress accuracy in your playing. Work in front of a mirror so you can see if your hand position and motion are accurate.

Always play any new material slowly until thoroughly learned. Only then can the fingers be properly trained to move quickly and smoothly while remaining relaxed.

60

Etude No. 3 **CD TRACK 28**
Play **very slowly** at first, counting in 3/4: "1 & 2 & 3 &."

Half Steps on the G (3rd) String

The following chromatic scale exercise includes G♯ and A♯ on the G (3rd) string. By what flat names could these notes also be called?

Begin your practice session by playing exercise 37 multiple times until you feel comfortable with these new notes. Practice in both **free stroke** and **rest stroke**.

Exercise 37

Keep the left fingers curved; hold them down when ascending. Keep right tip joints firm.
Alternate *i* and *m*, then *m* and *a*.

"Etude No. 4" includes G♯ and A on the 3rd string. Remember that a chromatic sign remains in effect for the remainder of the measure in which it appears; for example, G♯ is played throughout measures 3, 4, and 12.

Etude No. 4

Count **slowly** and **evenly**. Use free stroke, keeping the right hand relaxed and steady. Practice first with *i* and *m*, then with *m* and *a*; **do not neglect** *a*. Hold the left hand fingers down as shown by broken lines.

In "Prelude No. 8," observe the sharp (♯) just after the treble clef on the 5th line (F) of the staff. It indicates that whenever the note F appears in this piece, F♯ is played instead of F. The sharp signs in parentheses have been included as mere reminders and are not ordinarily found in music.

Do you know the meaning of **C** used as a time signature? (See p. 15.)

Prelude No. 8

Try first with fingers in rest stroke and thumb in free stroke, then practice with the fingers and thumb in free stroke.

Arpeggios

The exercises, etudes, and preludes in this section use *arpeggio* forms, meaning the recurrent figure in each measure contains the members of a complete chord, and they should, therefore, be played using free stroke with the fingers and thumb. The following concepts will help you develop habits of motion that will assist with arpeggios.

Sympathetic Motion

The concept of *sympathetic motion* is paramount to fluid and relaxed arpeggios. Sympathetic motion is the motion of fingers moving together, or "in sympathy," much like multiple pendulums swinging together create momentum that is far greater than any one of the parts moving on its own.

An example of sympathetic motion is illustrated in exercise 38, in which the thumb plays the bass while the fingers all move together in sympathetic motion to play the three upper voices. Remember to allow *c* to move sympathetically with *i, m,* and *a,* even though it is not playing a string; never hold *c* out or keep it stationary by holding it in. If *c* is moving sympathetically along with *a,* it will not become tense.

The approach for playing exercise 38 is as follows: Properly position the right hand by preparing the thumb on the 5th string with the fingers on the 3rd, 2nd, and 1st strings, as shown in figure 63. Play the bass note with *p* on beat 1 (fig. 64); on beat 2, play the fingers together in sympathy, and place *p* back on the bass string (fig. 65). When *p* plays the bass string again, the fingers will "reset" together and prepare on the appropriate strings (fig. 64). This alternating movement between *p* and sympathetic fingers *i, m,* and *a* is repeated, and is the basis for arpeggios. The motion is relaxed, giving the sensation of simply closing the hand when the fingers play.

Fig. 63   *Fig. 64*   *Fig. 65*

Exercise 38
Remember: as *p* plays, the sympathetic set of *i, m,* and *a* open and move back to their starting position, preparing on strings 3, 2, and 1.

Arpeggios Using Sympathetic Motion

To apply sympathetic motion to arpeggios, proceed as you did for exercise 38. Your hand position and the movement of your thumb and fingers will be the same, except that when the fingers play, they will play the notes in the upper voices consecutively instead of together. As the fingers play in order, the pull of *i* will pull in *m*, and the pull of *m* will pull in *a*. When the thumb plays again, it resets the fingers together so they can start their cycle over. Let's begin to study this concept by first using *p*, *i*, and *m* as utilized in "Etude No. 5."

Arpeggio Using *p*, *i*, *m* Consecutively

To play "Etude No. 5," begin by placing the hand as shown in figure 66.

Fig. 66

Next, play the bass note with *p* on beat 1 (fig. 67); *i* plays on beat 2 (fig. 68); as *i* plays, the pull of *i* pulls in *m* to play on beat 3 (fig. 69). Because *a* is not playing, it will move in and out sympathetically with *m*. As each finger plays the string, it continues to move inward to pull the subsequent finger until the final finger *m* plays, with *a* moving along sympathetically. As *m* plays, *p* resets on the next bass string (fig. 69).

Fig. 67

Fig. 68

Fig. 69

Etude No. 5 **CD TRACK 29**

Etude No. 5a
Be sure your fingers are moving sympathetically.

*Although the 3rd finger could be used here, start using the 4th finger as much as possible and reinforce the habit.

Arpeggio Using *p*, *i*, *m*, *a* Consecutively

To play exercise 39, begin by placing the hand as shown in figure 70.

Fig. 70

Next, play the bass note with *p* on beat 1 (fig. 71); *i* plays on the "&" of beat 1 (fig. 72); as *i* plays, the pull of *i* pulls in *m* to play on beat 2 (fig. 73); the pull of *m* pulls in *a* for the "&" of beat 2 (fig. 74). As each finger plays the string, it continues to move inward to pull the subsequent finger until the final finger *a* plays. At this point, *p* has reset on the bass string (fig. 74). When *p* plays, the fingers reset onto their respective strings together to start their next cycle (fig. 71).

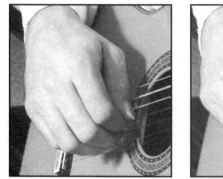   

Fig. 71   *Fig. 72*   *Fig. 73*   *Fig. 74*

At first, exercise 39 is played with fingers prepared, thus creating a slightly staccato sound. As fluency is acquired, the fingers will make contact only at their instance of playing and create a more legato arpeggio. Be sure that *c* follows *a* sympathetically and is not held still.

Exercise 39

Prelude No. 9

Arpeggio Using *p, i, m, a, m, i* Consecutively

Prepare to play exercise 40 by placing the hand as shown in figure 75.

Fig. 75

Next, play the bass note with *p* on beat 1 (fig. 76); *i* plays on the "&" of beat 1 (fig. 77); as *i* plays, the pull of *i* pulls in *m* to play on beat 2 (fig. 78); the pull of *m* pulls in *a* for the "&" of beat 2 (fig. 79). As each finger plays the string, it continues to move inward to pull the subsequent finger until *a* plays, and *m* and *i* are reset on their respective strings (fig. 79). Finger *m* plays on beat 3 (fig. 80); the pull of *m* brings *i* in to play on the "&" of beat 3, and *p* is reset on the bass string (fig. 81). When *p* plays, the fingers reset onto their respective strings together to start their next cycle (fig. 76). Note that there are two reset movements in this arpeggio form: when *p* plays and the fingers are reset (fig. 76), and when *a* plays and *m* and *i* are reset (fig. 79).

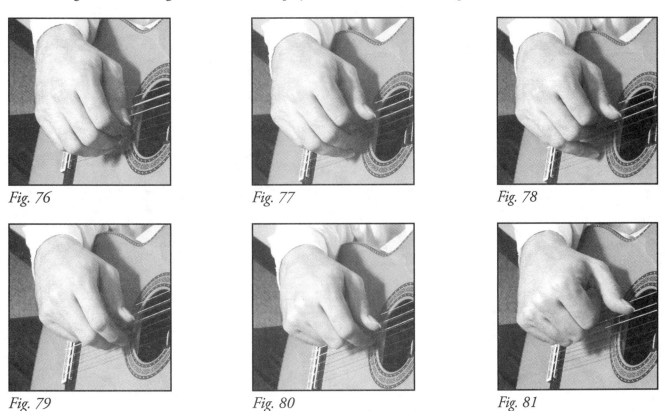

Fig. 76   *Fig. 77*   *Fig. 78*

Fig. 79   *Fig. 80*   *Fig. 81*

At first, exercise 40 is played with fingers prepared, thus creating a slightly staccato sound. As fluency is acquired, the fingers will only make contact at their instance of playing and create a more legato arpeggio.

Exercise 40
Be sure *c* moves sympathetically with *a*.

Prelude No. 10 **CD TRACK 30**

Notes on the D, or 4th, String

D	E	F
open	2nd fret	3rd fret
	2nd finger	3rd finger

  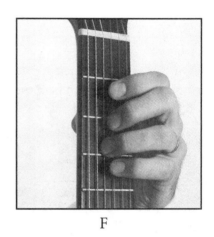

| D | E | F |

Be sure to preread, then, when comfortable, proceed to say and play each exercise. Careful alternation of *m* and *i*, then *m* and *a*, is essential. Practice in both free stroke and rest stroke.

Exercise 41

Exercise 42
Play **slowly** and **evenly**. Keep **left fingers curved** and **tip joints firm**.

Arpeggio Using *p*, *i*, *m*, *i* Consecutively

"Etude No. 6" is played in free stroke with both thumb and fingers. To begin, place the hand with *p* on the 5th string and *m* and *i* on the 3rd and 2nd, respectively (fig. 82).

Fig. 82

The sympathetic movement is similar to a *p*, *i*, *m* arpeggio (figs. 83 & 84), but when *m* plays, *i* resets, thus causing a brief alternation between *i* and *m* (fig. 85). When *p* plays again (fig. 86), the fingers reset together (fig. 83). Remember that *a* and *c* will move sympathetically with *m*.

Fig. 83

Fig. 84

Fig. 85

Fig. 86

Important!

1. Check the arch of your right wrist.
2. Be sure you are in free stroke position.
3. Hand is steady and not bouncing.
4. Fingers follow through.
5. Keep *c* down; follow through with *a*, which follows *m* sympathetically.

Etude No. 6

"Prelude No. 11" introduces a new time signature, $\frac{6}{8}$. How is it counted? (See p. 15.)

In "Prelude No. 11," *m* and *i* work sympathetically in free stroke. As *i* makes its stroke, *m* must execute a follow-through movement; both fingers will extend to playing position when *p* makes its stroke. Be sure *a* and *c* follow *m*. Also practice with *a* and *m*, applying the same principles. With *p, a, m,* the *i* finger will follow *m* sympathetically.

Carefully observe the left hand fingering; the 4th finger is used for G on the 1st string and D on the 2nd string.

Prelude No. 11
Play **slowly** and **carefully**. Be sure your fingers follow through.

Carefully practice "Moorish Dance" with just the bass part first. When comfortable, incorporate the treble part. Be sure to work in small segments, such as two measures at a time, and preread, then say and play. Play **slowly** until learned. Use a metronome, and count out loud.

Important!

1. Check the arch of your right wrist.

2. Be sure you are in free stroke position.

3. Hand is steady and not bouncing.

4. Fingers follow through; *i*, *a*, and *c* move with *m*.

Moorish Dance

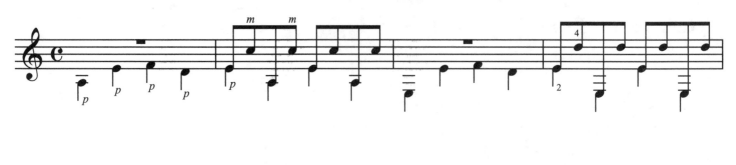

Tremolo

The *p, a, m, i* movement introduced in "Prelude No. 12" is used to play the beautiful tremolo compositions often heard in recitals and recordings. In a manner similar to that of "Prelude No. 11," *a* and *m* must, each in turn, execute a follow-through until *i* plays. Fingers *a*, *m*, and *i* move sympathetically inward until *p* plays, when they are then reset to playing position. Emphasize the extension of the fingers as *p* makes its stroke (figs. 87–91).

Caution: *a*, *m*, and *i* must be even and balanced with each other. Also, be sure *c* is following *a*.

Fig. 87: *p* on 5th string, *a* on 2nd string

Fig. 88: *p* plays 5th string

Fig. 89: *a* plays, *m* prepares on 2nd string

Fig. 90: *m* plays, *i* prepares on 2nd string

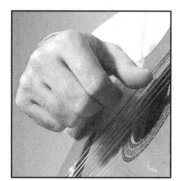
Fig. 91: *i* plays, *p* prepares on 5th string

Prelude No. 12

Half Steps on the D (4th) String

Exercise 43 is a chromatic scale exercise that includes the notes D♯ and F♯ on the 4th string. What are the flat names of these notes?

The chromatic exercises in this book are a very important part of your daily study. When ascending, make a concentrated effort to hold **all** the left fingers down until changing to the next string. Play exercise 43 at the beginning of each practice session, until your fingers are free and warmed up.

Exercise 43

Notes on the A, or 5th, String

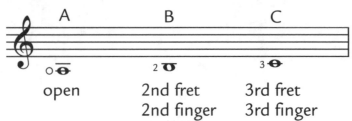

A	B	C

Exercise 44
Preread, then say and play each note until all are thoroughly learned. Use free stroke with *p*.

Etude No. 7 **CD TRACK 31**

Count slowly. Preread in segments, then say and play each segment. Play slowly to avoid confusion and error. Practice with fingers in both free and rest stroke.

Exercise 45

First play with *p* until the left hand fingering is executed with confidence; then, thoroughly practice with *i* and *m* alternation, first in rest stroke, then in free stroke.

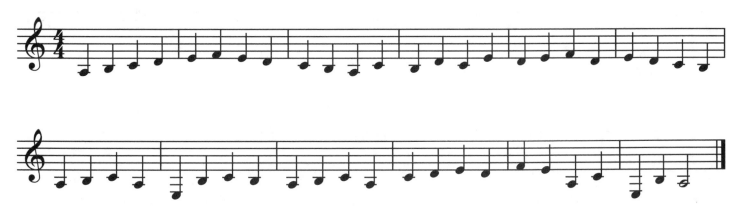

Prelude No. 13

Measures containing eighth notes should be isolated and practiced separately,
especially where *i* and *a* are used. **Count slowly and evenly.**

Notes on the E, or 6th, String

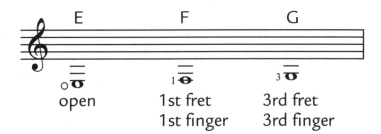

E	F	G
open	1st fret	3rd fret
	1st finger	3rd finger

| E | F | G |

The instructions given for exercise 45 (p. 75) should be carefully followed when studying exercise 46. Preread, then say and play until you feel comfortable with the new notes.

Exercise 46

About Practicing

How you practice is the single most important factor in your study of music and the guitar. With enough time, thoughtful practice habits, applied regularly each day, will assure you of success. Anyone can learn to play the guitar well who sincerely desires to do so.

The bass part of "Etude No. 8" should first be studied alone until it can be played very freely and evenly; then the treble part may be included easily to form the complete composition. Carefully observe the chromatic signs (accidentals): 4th-string D♯ and 1st-string F♯ in measure 2, and 5th-string C♯ in measure 6. Remember to preread, and then say and play.

Etude No. 8   **CD TRACK 32**

Exercise 47

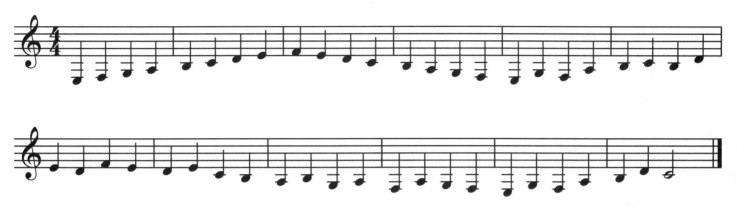

If the rhythm of "Prelude No. 14" is broken by difficulty encountered in the third measure, practice it separately until it flows. Always do isolations before playing through a piece.

Prelude No. 14   **CD TRACK 33**

The Right Hand in Long Scales

Maintaining the correct hand position when crossing strings in long scale passages requires careful analysis and training. This demands concentration on two functions:

1. The hand must correctly cross the strings at an angle, actually describing a slight arc, while **the elbow is used as the sole pivot point**, and the proper position of hand-to-arm is maintained. Crossing the strings in this manner eliminates the complicated, unstable piston-like action of the arm sliding back and forth along the edge of the guitar.

2. When playing a descending scale, the hand must be lifted sufficiently to maintain the correct position with the fingers. There is often a strong tendency not to lift the hand enough when the 5th and 6th strings are reached, forcing the fingers to curl under the hand in an awkward, tension-inducing position.

Notice that the elbow is more flexed when playing on the 6th string (fig. 92) and more extended when playing on the 1st string (fig. 93).

Fig. 92

Fig. 93

Memorize the step-wise progression of natural notes in exercise 48, and carefully observe the points of technique just explained. Use this example as a warm-up exercise every day, constantly striving to perfect the smoothness and accuracy of the right hand and arm movement when crossing the strings.

Remember! Pivot from the elbow when crossing strings.

Exercise 48
Use *i* and *m*, then *m* and *a,* in both free stroke and rest stroke.

Exercise 49

Keep the left fingers curved. Play slowly, and be sure to alternate.

Use *i* and *m*, then *m* and *a,* in both free stroke and rest stroke.

"Etude No. 9" is an excellent study of the natural notes on all six strings.

The coordinated action of *p* and *i* is especially important when playing the type of figure found in the first and second measures: as *p* makes its stroke, *i* must extend downward to playing position; as *i* makes its stroke, *p* must lift back to playing position.

Employ free stroke with both the thumb and fingers. Keep the **right hand relaxed and steady!** Play **slowly** until you feel comfortable.

Note: The last line of this piece has a repeat sign with *1st and 2nd endings*, indicated by the numerals 1 and 2 under brackets above the staff. Play through the first ending, and on the repeat, skip the first ending and play the second ending instead.

Etude No. 9 CD TRACK 34

Two Notes Played Together

The following five studies are examples of two notes played simultaneously. The fingers play in rest stroke, and thumb in free stroke. **Correctly relaxed finger and thumb action is extremely important!** Repeat each study until the fingers and thumb coordinate smoothly and with a reasonable degree of relaxation. Play first with *p* and *i* together, then *p* and *m*, then *p* and *a*.

To preread or say and play simultaneous notes, say the notes from bottom to top in their rhythmic grouping: E–C, E–C, E–C, E–C | F–B, F–B, F–B, F–B, etc. Be sure to see where the notes are located on the guitar in your mind's eye.

In exercise 50, the fingers and thumb work closely together separated by only one string, and *i* and *p* must not bump together causing one to restrict the stroke of the other. This tendency is eliminated by extending *p* slightly farther forward (toward the fingerboard), and the fingers slightly backward.

Exercise 50

Exercise 51

Exercise 52

First apply strict alternation as marked, then alternate *m* and *i*, then *a* and *m*, and *m* and *a*. Play **slowly**. Keep the **right hand relaxed and steady**.

Etude No. 10

Etude No. 11

You are cautioned not to hurry through this material. The coordinated movements of the thumb and fingers must be carefully and thoroughly developed. Play slowly until comfortable.

Half Steps on the A (5th) and E (6th) Strings

Fig. 94

In exercise 53, the new notes are A♯ and C♯ on the 5th string, and F♯ and G♯ on the 6th string. What are the flat names of these notes?

Exercise 53 should be played from memory many times at the beginning of each practice session; it is an excellent study for both hands. It is interesting to observe that in playing this chromatic scale exercise, the 4th finger is used on all strings except the 3rd string.

Important! The right hand instructions for exercise 48 (p. 80) must be applied to exercise 53.

Exercise 53
Keep the left fingers curved throughout, and hold them down when ascending.

Note: A number in a circle indicates the string.

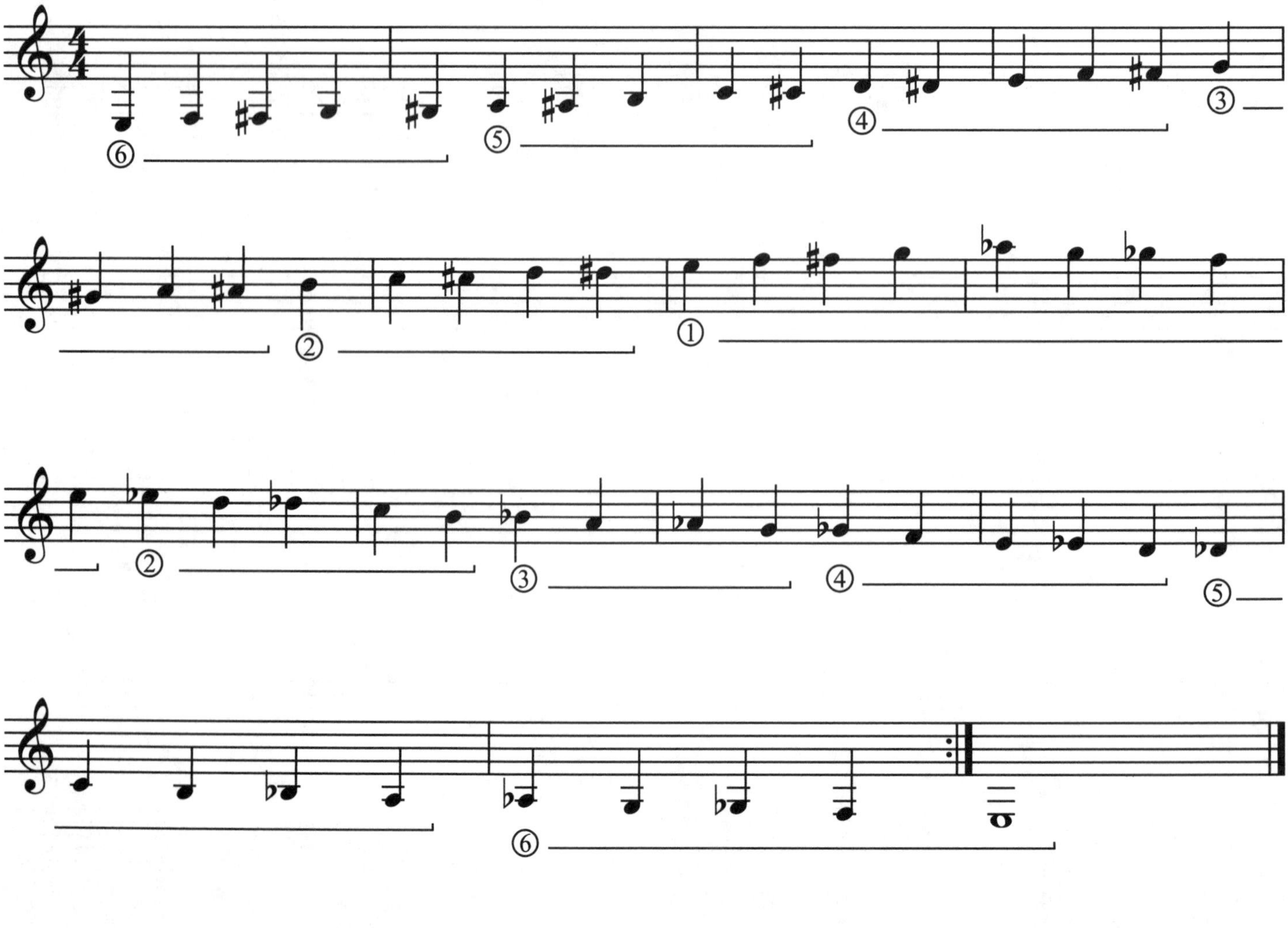

"Folk Song" includes three sharps just after the clef sign: 1st-string F♯, 2nd-string C♯, and 3rd-string G♯. Locate them on your guitar. **Remember**, when any of these three notes appear in this composition, they must be played sharp, except in measure 12 where G is marked with a natural sign.

Play the melody (treble part) alone until thoroughly familiar with the notes and rhythm; then play both treble and bass parts together as written. Strictly alternate *i* and *m* using the rest stroke. Play **slowly**, and **count evenly**.

Note: *D.C. al Fine* at the end of the last line means to repeat from the beginning of the composition and stop at *Fine*. (Consult a music dictionary for the full meaning and pronunciation.)

Folk Song

CD TRACK 35

Another method of sounding two notes together is with the fingers, while *p* again assumes a position of rest to support the hand.

Observe that only the **free stroke** is possible when playing two notes together **on adjacent strings**.

Play exercise 54 first with *m* and *i* together—*m* for the higher string, *i* for the lower—then practice thoroughly with *a* and *m*, for the higher and lower strings, respectively. Realize that *m* and *i* are moving sympathetically.

Remember! A chromatic sign is effective for the remainder of the measure in which it appears.

Exercise 54
Play **slowly**, carefully observing the basic principles of finger action. Keep the **right hand relaxed and steady!**

Again, you are advised not to rush the process of learning the guitar. The speed of your progress depends upon the amount of thoughtful practice you apply each day. Still, it takes time to develop the mind and muscles correctly for playing this responsive instrument. You should experience much enjoyment from good practice; you have already been richly rewarded! Have faith that the full extent of your aspirations can be realized with time and patient effort.

Prelude No. 15
Always remember to preread and say and play.

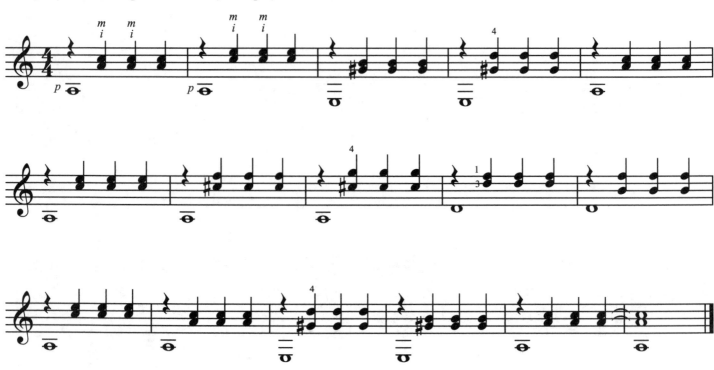

Count "Country Dance" slowly and evenly.

Country Dance

F. Carulli
1770–1841

The **right hand must remain relaxed and steady.** These compositions were intentionally written to be played slowly so that you can concentrate upon relaxation and accuracy.

Prelude No. 16

Play *p* in free stroke. Remember to play F♯ throughout the entire composition.

Allegro

F. Carulli

Three Notes Played Together

For exercise 55, apply the instructions given for exercise 54, except now use *a*, *m*, and *i* together.

Due to its natural weakness, special attention should be directed to *a* in this case. The highest "voice" of a three-note chord played with the fingers is always sounded by *a* and must be struck with sufficient force to be heard distinctly. Realize that *a*, *m*, and *i* are moving sympathetically.

When prereading or saying and playing three notes together, say the notes from bottom to top in their rhythmic grouping: G–B–E, G–B–E, G–B–E, G–B–E, etc. Be sure to see where the notes are located on the guitar in your mind's eye.

The following familiar reminder is repeated here because of its extreme importance: keep the **right fingertip segments firm**, and the **hand very steady**.

Exercise 55

Carefully observe the chromatic signs (accidentals) in "Prelude No. 17": A♯ and C♯ on the 5th string, and C♯ on the 2nd string. The natural sign appears in measures 13 and 19.

Prelude No. 17
Play **slowly** and **evenly**. Keep **right hand steady**. **Preread**, then **say and play**.

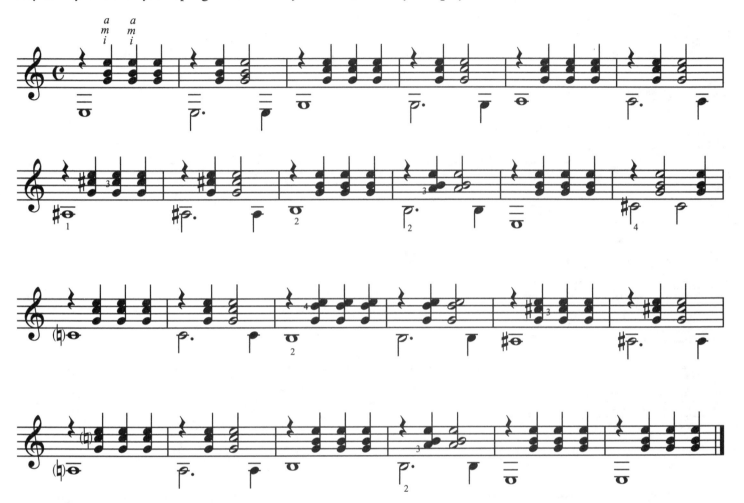

Suggestions for Most Beneficial Practice

The difficulty of playing accurately *and* fast increases with the distance the fingers are lifted away from the strings, so never lift them higher than necessary; this rule applies to **both hands**.

Whatever your aspirations with the guitar may be, you must not neglect daily practice of scale and arpeggio exercises. Begin each practice session by playing chromatic scale exercise 43 (p. 74) **slowly and forcefully** so that proper finger movement of both hands can be carefully established. Then, after the fingers become invigorated and free, practice light and fast, but not so fast that the fingers become tense, thereby sacrificing evenness. After exercise 43, play exercise 53 many times. Do not neglect the training of *a* in scales.

After practicing the scale exercises, practice various *arpeggio formulas,* especially the *p, i, m, a, m, i* movement in "Prelude No. 10" (p. 68), and the *p, m, i, a, m, a* movement in "Prelude No. 17a" (p. 92). Again, play slowly and forcefully at first, then lightly and quickly as the finger action becomes free. Make certain, however, that every note of the arpeggio is distinct and in even rhythm; arpeggios should always **flow**.

When you finish this routine, the fingers will be "warmed" to their task of playing, and you will be able to more beneficially apply yourself to the problems of becoming a better musician and guitarist.

The important new arpeggio formula *p, m, i, a, m, a* is introduced in "Prelude No. 17a."

A word of caution regarding one extremely important point of right hand technique: **the first (basal) segment of a finger must always perform a slight follow-through instantly after the string is sounded.** When playing arpeggios, the first segment *often tends to jerk outward during the stroke* instead of following in the same general direction as the middle and tip segments move. Besides creating tension, this action produces a very weak tone. Again, you are urged to carefully check your finger movements—**especially** for *a*—with the aid of a mirror.

Prelude No. 17a

Pivot Fingers and Guide Fingers
Important Principles of Left Hand Technique

A *pivot finger* is a left hand finger that remains stationary while other fingers move to new notes.
A *guide finger* is a finger that does not entirely leave the string when moving up or down to a new note.

The use of guide fingers is illustrated in measures 2 and 3 of "Prelude No. 18," where the 2nd and 3rd fingers remain lightly upon their respective strings and shift the distance of one fret to the next chord. Using guide fingers greatly simplifies shifting to another chord position, and this technique should be developed and used whenever practical in playing all music for the guitar.

In "Prelude No. 18," observe that the **2nd finger remains on the 3rd string** at either the 2nd or 1st fret throughout the first 16 measures, serving either as a *guide* or a *pivot* (measure 11) for placing the other fingers. The foregoing is an application of the familiar rule: **never lift a finger until necessary**. Remember to preread, and say and play.

Prelude No. 18

Prelude No. 18a
The study of arpeggios must not be neglected because they are present in almost all guitar music. "Prelude No. 18" becomes an excellent arpeggio study simply by playing the chords as arpeggios. Apply the same arpeggio pattern used in "Prelude No. 10," as shown here.

General Use of the Two Different Stroke Types

You may have already observed that the rest stroke facilitates the execution of rapid scale passages and also produces broader tone and greater volume than does the free stroke. While there are exceptions, it is possible to state, in general terms, where each of the two strokes may be used.

When to Use Rest Stroke

1. Any part requiring special emphasis, such as the melody
   (usually found in either the treble or bass part of a composition)

2. Scales or scale passages

When to Use Free Stroke

1. Arpeggios

2. Chords

3. Scale passages in which rest stroke is neither practical nor desirable

4. Parts that do not require special emphasis

Keep in mind that the foregoing rules are of a general nature only. The use of the strokes varies in accordance with the spirit and character of a composition. The ability to employ the correct stroke at any given time requires a high degree of musicianship and technical development.

Rest Stroke with the Thumb

The next step in the study of classic guitar technique pertains to playing two notes together, using the free stroke with the fingers and the rest stroke with the thumb. The development of the rest stroke with *p* is an important area of guitar technique; it is also a difficult stroke to execute properly. Students who aspire to reach higher levels of guitar virtuosity and musicianship cannot neglect this technical necessity.

Etudes 7, 8, and 9, and Preludes 14 and 15 have bass notes that sound alone. These examples should be practiced—preferably from memory—focusing full attention on the right hand and *p*.

Caution! Maintain the correctly tilted hand position as shown in figure 23 on page 23. **Do not, in any case, allow the hand to follow its natural inclination to roll to the right.** To facilitate execution of the rest stroke with *p*, however, it is permissible to arch the wrist **slightly** and be sure that *p* comes to rest on the adjacent string (figs. 95 & 96).

Fig. 95

Fig. 96

Exercise 56

First, practice the bass part of exercise 56 alone, counting **very evenly**; then play both parts together.
Remember: rest stroke with *p*, and free stroke with the fingers. Play **slow, relaxed, and even.**

Exercise 56a

Here, the 1st and 2nd strings are played in reverse order. Thoroughly practice the finger formulas *m* and *i*, then *a* and *m*.

etc.

The Importance of Reviewing

Students are advised to review the various sections of this book frequently until they are mastered; otherwise, the "touch" of certain movements might be lost. A qualified guitarist must be able to execute any movement fluently at any time, in accordance with the demands of the music. Therefore, sections that presented difficulties must be thoroughly reviewed again and again.

Free Stroke with the Thumb and Fingers

Now we will focus on executing the free stroke with both the thumb and fingers simultaneously. This particular movement is employed when playing adjacent strings together and in playing chords; it is quite simple and natural if the hand is held properly relaxed and steady.

At this time, you are well acquainted with the two different positions of the hand that are necessary to play:

1. fingers rest stroke, *p* free stroke
2. fingers free stroke, *p* rest stroke

The hand position for playing free stroke with both *p* and the fingers simultaneously is approximately midway between the two strokes named above. Remember to extend *p* forward (toward the fingerboard) and the fingers backward (toward the bridge) in all movements such as this, where they must work closely together. (See instructions for exercise 50 on page 84.)

Play this short example until coordination of *p* and each finger is achieved.

When playing exercise 57, the right hand must be relaxed and steady, with plucking movement coming from *p* and fingers only: thus, the natural tendency of the hand to "fly" outward is minimized.

Exercise 57
Play **slowly** and **evenly.** Use *p* for lower notes, and fingers for upper notes.

Exercise 58
Use *i* and *m* for the two upper notes, and *p* for the bottom note.

Exercise 59

Carefully study with *p* and each of the fingers in free stroke, first with *i*, then *m*, then *a*.
Play **very slowly**; keep the **right hand relaxed and steady**. Also try with alternation (*i* and *m*, etc.).

Exercise 59a

Alternate *i* and *m*, then *m* and *i*, then *a* and *m*, then *m* and *a*. Play *p* in free stroke.

Exercise 60

Exercise 60 is a short scale study of repeated notes using the rest stroke. **Evenness** is most important!
Play **slow** and **firm**, then **light** and **fast**. Use strict alternation throughout, first with *i* and *m*, then *m* and *a*.

Exercise 61

Use rest stroke with fingers, free stroke with *p*.

Prelude No. 19

Use strict alternation of *m* and *i* throughout.

Four Notes Played Together

When playing four notes together (free stroke with the thumb and fingers simultaneously), the right hand is held in a very relaxed free stroke position. Special effort is required to maintain alignment at the wrist (see fig. 15 on p. 22). The **right hand and arm must remain steady**; all movement comes from *p* and the fingers. Be sure to follow through inward so the hand does not bounce up.

Exercise 62
Play **very slowly** at first.

In "Etude No. 12," the highest voice of each chord is regarded as a melody note; it must be sounded with sufficient force—by *a*—to be distinctly heard. Most students find it necessary to stress the stroke of *a* until the finger becomes accustomed to its task.

Carefully observe left hand fingering; **never lift a finger until necessary.**

Remember: the easiest way to play any composition is to isolate and thoroughly practice difficult passages.

Etude No. 12

Waltz

F. Carulli

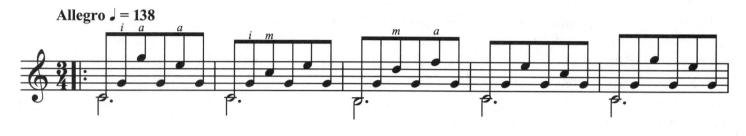

All the single melody notes in "Prelude No. 20" are played rest stroke. Practically no change in hand position is required to play rest stroke in this case; the fingers merely extend forward to play the single notes. **The right hand *and* arm must remain relaxed and steady.**

The musical texture created when chords are followed or preceded by single notes is very widely used in all types of guitar music; therefore, the following piece should be studied most thoroughly. It is not to be played fast. Emphasis must be placed upon **evenness** and the training of *a* to sound the melody note of each chord distinctly. Carefully observe the fingering for each hand.

Prelude No. 20
Preread, then **say and play**.

Using Rest Stroke and Free Stroke to Emphasize Melody

This section explains a particular movement of the right hand fingers used to emphasize the melody of a composition. This requires that a **rest stroke** with one finger be immediately followed by a **free stroke** with another finger. For the purpose of explanation, complex passages involving the use of both types of stroke are marked with two easily identified signs placed above or below the notes:

    Rest stroke is indicated by ▽.

    Free stroke is indicated by ∪.

Repeat exercises 63 and 63a many times, with careful attention to stroke markings. When executing the free stroke, be sure the tip segment of *i* maintains its firmness. Play **very slowly**.

Exercise 63   *Exercise 63a*

Prelude No. 21

Play slowly until learned, then moderately fast. *D.S. al Fine* means to repeat from the sign 𝄋 and end at *Fine*.

Andantino

M. Carcassi
1792–1853

English Dance

F. Carulli

Music of the Masters

The four composers represented by the short pieces that follow were the greatest guitarists of their time. Not only were they great instrumentalists, they were excellent composers as well. The fact that their compositions regularly appear in contemporary recordings and concerts all over the world is evidence of the quality of their music. Each dedicated himself to the task of improving the technique of playing the guitar and establishing a better system of teaching it. Their written method books, while incomplete in the light of present-day technique, are considered worthwhile contributions to literature for study of the guitar. Each of these masters helped to elevate the instrument to its present respected position in the world of music.

Of even greater value is the unquestionably rich treasure of studies and concert pieces left to us by these men. Each composer wrote a tremendous number of works, which ranged in difficulty from easy little etudes to compositions requiring the highest degree of proficiency. While the following selections belong to the first category, each one is a complete musical composition. Some are tuneful with the harmonic support necessary for contrast and color, and others are arpeggio studies requiring fast, even execution with both hands for proper interpretation.

Proper study of these works is most helpful for students to develop musically as well as technically. You may be assured that, by carefully learning to play each composition, you will better equip yourself to progress toward larger works of even richer musical content.

You are urged to memorize those of the following pieces that appeal to you most, and not to hesitate about performing them for everyone interested in listening. It is a privilege to be able to play the guitar and its music. The author strongly suggests that one should share one's good fortune with others.

Ferdinand Carulli

Ferdinand Carulli was born in Naples, Italy, on February 10, 1770, and he died in Paris, France, on February 17, 1841. He was a famous guitar virtuoso, composer, and musical author. He received his first training from a priest, and after several years of persistent study, gained recognition in Naples as a performer and teacher. He moved to Leghorn in 1797, where he soon became established as a virtuoso and teacher. His concert performances were so successful locally that soon after the turn of the century he began touring Europe. The wide acclaim he received in Paris caused him, in 1808, to make that city his permanent home. During the remaining 33 years of his life, he did not leave France for any long period of time, choosing rather to be "in residence" as a concert master, teacher, and composer until his death in 1841.

Waltz and Three Variations

F. Carulli

CD TRACK 36

This waltz and variations is from Carulli's "method" published in 1810. To obtain maximum benefit from this work, first study each section slowly and thoroughly with careful attention to fingering. The tempo may be subsequently increased, but never to a degree that the composition sounds hurried or evenness of execution is sacrificed.

Fernando Sor

Fernando Sor was born in Barcelona, Spain, on February 14, 1778. He died in Paris, France, on July 8, 1839. He was one of the greatest guitarists and composers of all time. The thorough instruction he received in music theory and composition at a Barcelona monastery provided the foundation upon which he built his career. At the age of 17, already an accomplished guitarist and composer, he wrote a successful opera. His impact upon the music world was particularly notable in England, where he journeyed in 1809 and his efforts caused the guitar to become immensely popular. Needless to say, he soon became recognized throughout all of Europe as a master of the guitar and an extraordinary composer. Sor wrote an incredible number of musical compositions—over 400 in all. His works include opera, oratorios, symphonies, quartets, and church music. His guitar compositions are of such excellence that even today they appear on numerous recordings and in practically all concert programs of the leading contemporary guitarists.

The first section (16 bars) of "Andante I" by Sor is played entirely in free stroke. (See page 102 for the meaning of the ▽ and ◡ signs.) Measures 17–24 require a combination of both the free stroke and the rest stroke; melody notes with stems pointing up are played rest stroke, and notes with stems pointing down are played free stroke. The last eight measures of the piece are primarily a repetition of the beginning and played in the same manner as the first section.

Observe the $\frac{3}{8}$ time signature indicating that an eighth note receives one beat. A quarter note, therefore, receives two beats. The entire piece should be played with a steady, even "1–2–3" count. Practice slowly at first.

The Italian word *andante* is used in music to indicate a very moderate tempo. Therefore, any composition marked *andante* must never be played fast, but instead at an easy, moving pace.

Andante I

F. Sor

CD TRACK 37

The first eight measures of "Andante II" by Sor is played using free stroke for both the melody and bass parts. In measures 9–24, the rest stroke is used for all melody notes, and free stroke is used for the bass.

Andante II

F. Sor

Allegretto is an Italian word used in music to indicate a rather light and cheerful tempo, but not fast. *Allegro* means fast or rapid. *Allegretto* is faster than *andante,* but slower than *allegro.*

"Allegretto I" should be played as legato (smoothly) as possible. It consists of three, sometimes four, parts or voices. Practice slowly, counting evenly, increasing the tempo only after well learned. Carefully analyze each part separately, and observe the manner in which notes and rests form a measure. Be sure to preread, and say and play.

Allegretto I

CD TRACK 39

F. Sor

"Allegretto II" is considered a two-voice composition. The treble part contains some rather difficult right hand fingering; it must therefore be studied carefully. Note that when a finger is repeated, it begins a three-note figure (curved lines in the music indicate some examples). The entire treble part is played rest stroke, except for beat 1 of measure 24 and beat 3 of measure 30. All bass notes are played free stroke.

Allegretto II

CD TRACK 40

F. Sor

Mauro Giuliani

Mauro Giuliani was born in Bologna, Italy, in 1781 and died in Vienna in 1829. His education in music began at an early age, and the violin and flute were the first practical application of his studies. While still a youth, he entirely discarded those two instruments and began a serious and intense study of the guitar. He was, for the most part, self-taught. So extraordinary was his genius, however, that by the time he reached the age of 18, he had begun touring Europe as a virtuoso. More amazing still, he had already composed a number of brilliant compositions for the guitar. Throughout his life, he associated with the greatest musicians of his day, all of whom held him in the highest esteem. It is said that Beethoven, after hearing him play, exclaimed, "The guitar is a miniature orchestra in itself." Giuliani wrote over 300 compositions, which ranged in difficulty from easy exercises to works requiring a high degree of technical skill. His compositions still appear in the concert programs and recordings of our foremost guitarists.

The beginning 16 measures of the "Andantino" by Giuliani introduces a melody (theme) supported by one lower voice line. Both are played with the free stroke. The melody is repeated in the next 16 measures, but with the full harmonic support of two lower voices. In the three-part section, the melody is played rest stroke and the two lower parts free stroke. Due to the complexity of this section in three parts, it is strongly recommended that each part be analyzed and practiced separately before attempting to play them together as written. The entire composition must be played at the same tempo, the first 16 measures no faster than the last.

Andantino is another Italian word. When used as the name of a composition, it indicates a short piece of *andante* tempo and character.

Andantino

M. Giuliani

CD TRACK 41

110

The title "Allegro" indicates that the tempo of this composition is rapid, but if it is to be played well, it must be practiced very slowly at first. This is an excellent study for the development of both hands. Carefully observe all finger markings. Preread, and say and play.

Allegro

M. Giuliani

Dionisio Aguado

Dionisio Aguado was born in Madrid, Spain, on April 8, 1784, where he died on December 20, 1849. His first instruction was at a college in Madrid, where the monks taught him music theory and the elements of the guitar. Later, Manuel Garcia, who became a world-famous singer, instructed the young Aguado in the more advanced phases of guitar technique. He became a brilliant virtuoso who, according to no less an authority than Fernando Sor, played with extraordinary velocity and musicianship. Aguado produced several volumes of studies for the guitar that are of much value to the serious student of today. His advanced compositions are extremely difficult because they contain numerous passages requiring brilliant execution—the kind of playing in which the composer excelled. His "method," which has never been published in English, contains many excellent studies for the advanced student of the guitar.

All melody notes in "Waltz" by Aguado are played rest stroke except for the three-note chord in measure 16, and in measures 21, 22, and 23.

Observe the $\frac{3}{8}$ time signature indicating that an eighth note receives one beat. Where sixteenth notes appear (as on the second beat of measure 5), the measure is counted "1 2& 3."

After it is thoroughly learned, this composition should be played at a bright waltz tempo.

Waltz

D. Aguado

CD TRACK 43

Estudio is a Spanish word meaning "study." The following "Estudio" by Aguado is an excellent arpeggio study.

Measures 3 and 19 of this composition require some explanation. The note B is played on the 3rd string, as indicated by the circled numeral 3. (In guitar music, a number enclosed by a circle always indicates the string, and plain numbers indicate left hand fingers.) Besides being the name of the open 2nd string, the B on the third line of the staff is also found on the 3rd string, 4th fret, as we have learned from tuning the guitar.

Carefully observe left hand fingering, and note the extensive use of guide fingers.

This piece must be played very evenly, and, after thoroughly learned, at an *allegro* tempo (quite fast).

CD TRACK 44

Estudio

D. Aguado

Accompaniments for Exercises

Exercises 1 & 11   CD TRACKS 1 & 9

Exercises 2 & 12   CD TRACKS 2 & 10

Exercises 3 & 13 CD TRACKS 3 & 11

Exercises 4 & 14 CD TRACKS 4 & 12

Exercise 5 CD TRACK 5

Exercise 5 (cont.)

Exercise 6   **CD TRACK 6**

Exercise 7   **CD TRACK 7**

Exercise 8 CD TRACK 8

Exercise 15 CD TRACK 13

Exercise 16 CD TRACK 14

Exercise 17 CD TRACK 15

Exercise 18 CD TRACK 16

Exercise 19 CD TRACK 17

Exercise 22 **CD TRACK 19**

Exercise 23 **CD TRACK 23**

Using the Enhanced CD

The included *Classic Guitar Technique*, Vol. 1, companion CD provides demonstration tracks as well as accompaniment tracks to practice and play with when a teacher is not available. Tracks 1–35 correlate with exercises, etudes, and preludes found throughout the book, with background accompaniment and performances of both guitar parts for duets. Tracks 36–44 contain full performances of all the selections in the "Music of the Masters" section.

Counting is provided on the first 12 tracks to assist you in developing the habit of counting out loud. On subsequent tracks, you should continue the habit of counting to reinforce your sense of meter.

The tempos are slow and subdivided at first, so that security and confidence can be developed while minimizing confusion and error. Tempos on subsequent examples will speed up as your proficiency is developed.

The TNT (Tone 'N' Tempo) Changer software on this CD is compatible with both Mac and Windows and offers many features that allow you to customize your practicing experience. You can use the software to loop entire songs or isolate sections for playback, slow down and speed up the tempo without changing the pitch, and mute the solo guitar part to play along with just accompaniment as if with a teacher. For complete instructions, please see the TNT ReadMe.pdf file on the enhanced CD.

The recordings of the pieces in the "Music of the Masters" section are intended to give you the experience of an interpretive performance in a concert hall setting. These selections were performed by Thomas Kikta on a 1987 Thomas Humphrey Millennium, and recorded in Duquesne University's PNC Recital Hall using Bruel & Kjaer 4006 microphones.

CD Tracks

Track 1 ....Exercise 1
Track 2 ....Exercise 2
Track 3 ....Exercise 3
Track 4 ....Exercise 4
Track 5 ....Exercise 5
Track 6 ....Exercise 6
Track 7 ....Exercise 7
Track 8 ....Exercise 8
Track 9 ....Exercise 11
Track 10 ....Exercise 12
Track 11 ....Exercise 13
Track 12 ....Exercise 14
Track 13 ....Exercise 15
Track 14 ....Exercise 16
Track 15 ....Exercise 17
Track 16 ....Exercise 18
Track 17 ....Exercise 19
Track 18 ....Prelude No. 1
Track 19 ....Exercise 22
Track 20 ....Prelude No. 2
Track 21 ....Prelude No. 3
Track 22 ....Prelude No. 4
Track 23 ....Exercise 23
Track 24 ....Prelude No. 5
Track 25 ....Etude No. 1

Track 26 ....Prelude No. 6
Track 27 ....Etude No. 2
Track 28 ....Etude No. 3
Track 29 ....Etude No. 5
Track 30 ....Prelude No. 10
Track 31 ....Etude No. 7
Track 32 ....Etude No. 8
Track 33 ....Prelude No. 14
Track 34 ....Etude No. 9
Track 35 ....Folk Song
Track 36 ....Waltz and Three Variations
Track 37 ....Andante I
Track 38 ....Andante II
Track 39 ....Allegretto I
Track 40 ....Allegretto II
Track 41 ....Andantino
Track 42 ....Allegro
Track 43 ....Waltz
Track 44 ....Estudio
Track 45 ....Tuning Track: E (6th) String
Track 46 ....Tuning Track: A (5th) String
Track 47 ....Tuning Track: D (4th) String
Track 48 ....Tuning Track: G (3rd) String
Track 49 ....Tuning Track: B (2nd) String
Track 50 ....Tuning Track: E (1st) String